W9-AEQ-503

THE ART OF

SCORING

THE ART OF
SCORING

· ·

The Ultimate On-Course Guide
to Short Game Strategy and
Technique

Stan Utley
with Matthew Rudy

GOTHAM
BOOKS

GOTHAM BOOKS

Published by Penguin Group (USA) Inc.

375 Hudson Street, New York, New York 10014, U.S.A.

Penguin Group (Canada), 90 Eglinton Avenue East, Suite 700, Toronto, Ontario M4P 2Y3, Canada
(a division of Pearson Penguin Canada Inc.); Penguin Books Ltd, 80 Strand, London WC2R 0RL,
England; Penguin Ireland, 25 St Stephen's Green, Dublin 2, Ireland (a division of Penguin Books Ltd);
Penguin Group (Australia), 250 Camberwell Road, Camberwell, Victoria 3124, Australia (a division
of Pearson Australia Group Pty Ltd); Penguin Books India Pvt Ltd, 11 Community Centre, Panchsheel
Park, New Delhi – 110 017, India; Penguin Group (NZ), 67 Apollo Drive, Rosedale, North Shore 0632,
New Zealand (a division of Pearson New Zealand Ltd); Penguin Books (South Africa) (Pty) Ltd,
24 Sturdee Avenue, Rosebank, Johannesburg 2196, South Africa

Penguin Books Ltd, Registered Offices: 80 Strand, London WC2R 0RL, England

Published by Gotham Books, a member of Penguin Group (USA) Inc.

First printing, September 2009
10 9 8 7 6 5 4 3 2 1

Photos by J. D. Cuban

Gotham Books and the skyscraper logo are trademarks of Penguin Group (USA) Inc.

LIBRARY OF CONGRESS CATALOGING-IN-PUBLICATION DATA

Utley, Stan.
    The art of scoring: the ultimate on-course guide to short game strategy and technique by Stan Utley
with Matthew Rudy.
        p. cm.
    ISBN 978-1-592-40448-3 (hardcover)
    1. Short game (Golf)   I. Rudy, Matthew.   II. Title.
    GV979.S54U86 2009
    796.352'3—dc22   2009012029

Printed in the United States of America
Set in Augustal

CONTENTS

· ·

FOREWORD

by Jim Hardy

I've known Stan Utley for six years—since before he became a full-time teacher. When we first met, Stan had started to help Jay Haas and Peter Jacobsen with their putting, and Peter kept telling Stan about me, and the work I had been doing on the full swing with various tour players over the years.

Stan finally made a trip out to Houston to look for some help with his long game, and I offered to trade him full-swing lessons if he would help me with my putting.

It was a match made in heaven.

What Stan tries to get people to do with their putting and short game is consistent with what I want them to do with the full swing. We got along famously, right away—on a golf level, a personal level, and a faith level.

Leaving Stan's wonderful abilities as a teacher aside for a second, as a man, Stan's heart is in the right place. You will never meet anyone who makes you feel more comfortable, or who better understands the position you're in—in the game and in life. It's never about him. Stan is focused on helping YOU. When a teacher has that selfless quality, he's a real hero. When you couple that with Stan's expertise in the short game, and his talents as a teacher, it's a fantastic package.

Stan went from being a player with an elite skill to a person who wanted to teach that skill to others, and he developed a story-teller's talent for sharing. He asked his students to try some-thing, or to watch him as he demonstrated and described the way he did it. When he and I got together, and I started to explain what was happening in the swing, relative to swing plane and shaft angle and things like that, he immediately connected the dots.

Stan has an endearing, self-deprecating way about him, but he's also extraordinarily smart and catches on to concepts imme-diately. His short game expertise comes from his considerable experience as a player, and he combines this technical knowl-edge with his storytelling abilities to back up his "feel."

Harvey Penick was the classic anecdotal full-swing teacher—a man who taught by telling stories. But Harvey could also get as technical as you wanted to get. He just understood that there was a more effective way for most players to learn. Stan and I are in lockstep with Harvey there. I believe in giving a student the least amount of information necessary to get him to hit the ball well, and Stan has grown to be the same kind of instructor.

Stan has bridged the gap from being a player who under-stands the short game to an instructor who understands how to get these concepts across to a lot of different players. I've seen it firsthand, both in players I've watched him teach and with my own short game.

I was always very stubborn when it came to the short game. I believed that there were so many different successful styles of putting that I didn't need to be overly concerned about my setup as long as my putter moved more or less on an arc and the face of the putter stayed relatively square to that arc.

I believed that since the stroke wasn't very big and you weren't moving the ball very far, it wasn't particularly important whether you held the club cross-handed or stood open or closed to it. I fought getting my forearms square and parallel to the target line. It felt terrible. I couldn't aim. I didn't have any feel.

I was handicapping how good I could be with the putter.

After working with Stan, I can now really roll the ball—much better than I ever expected I'd be able to. He got me to feel the energy in the clubhead, and to understand that my hands didn't need to be involved in the hit. I could let the putting stroke happen—and that's infinitely easier to do when you stand to the ball correctly.

Stan showed me—and he'll show you here—that once you quit fighting your feel and get out of your own way, you can do incredible things around and on the green. Stan will show you a connection between your stroke and the putting line that you've never had before. A lot of people can get the putter—or a driver, or a 5-iron—in decent position at impact with a lot of compensation and recovery. We've all hit good putts before. But Stan shows you how to get in position to hit short game shots consistently well. Stan got me to believe what I already believed about the full swing, but with putting.

And after watching him with everyday-handicap players and with tour players, I'm so impressed with the wonderful, easy way he goes about his business. In my teaching, I'm a little harder-edged: I'll tell a player that if he listens to me, he's going to get better—and if he doesn't want to hear me out, he can go somewhere else. Stan will take your hand, and he'll be a cheerleader for you. He'll show you what to do, and he'll make you feel good about your progress. Sometimes, he'll help you succeed almost in spite of yourself. In his flair for relationships, Stan's a lot like Butch Harmon.

Stan is one of the highest-quality individuals I've ever met—I can't recommend him more highly to you, as a teacher or a friend. I'm certain the information he's going to share with you here will help you shoot better scores.

JIM HARDY

2007 PGA National Teacher of the Year

Author of the bestselling *The Plane Truth for Golfers*

Houston

November 2008

INTRODUCTION

. . . .

My goal is to help people have fun when they play golf.

It doesn't matter if you're Sergio Garcia trying to win a major championship or a 20-handicapper trying to get out of the bunker consistently. When I'm teaching you, I want you to get to a place where you enjoy the game, where you can't wait to play the next time.

The details might be different. Sergio wants to make five birdies a round and get up and down more than 65 percent of the time when he misses a green. You might want to play once a week, practice once a month, and break 90 consistently.

But there's a common thread: scoring.

Scoring comes from hitting the shot you meant to hit around and on the green. The number of times Sergio accomplishes it in a round might be different than the number of times you do, but the satisfaction is the same. If you're hitting more shots "on purpose"—and pulling them off—than you were before, your score is going to get better.

And you're going to have more fun.

Sure, you're saying to yourself. That's easy for him to say. Doing it is another thing.

Yes, but by the end of this book, you *will* be doing it—hitting virtually all the shots I teach to the two dozen tour players I work with week in and week out across the United States and Europe.

What is the "art of scoring"? I believe it's a kind of vision—a way of seeing the varieties of shots you can hit in a given situation. And I know from firsthand experience that it's vision you can learn. I'm going to show you how to "see" all the shots tour players see around and on the green, and how to pick the one that matches your skill level, confidence level, and risk tolerance.

If you're protecting a two-shot lead on the last hole of your club championship, you might want a nice, boring pitch shot that will leave you fifteen feet from the hole. Playing with some buddies in a skins game, you might want a high-risk/high-reward lofted shot, since there's no money for second place. We'll cover both options—and every shot in between.

For Chapter 1, I went out and played a round of golf with three amateurs—a 10-handicapper, a 15-handicapper, and a 20-handicapper—and guided them on what short game shots they should pick in certain situations. I think you'll be amazed at the improvement—with no changes whatsoever to their full swings.

Most players have at least a rough idea of their overall handicap. But do you know where you stand, skill-wise, on pitches and chips, sand play, trouble shots and putting? In Chapter 2, I'll show you how to determine a handicap-like grade for each part of your short game. That way, you'll know exactly which parts of this book are going to help you the most.

Chapter 3 is devoted to the three bread-and-butter shots I think every player has to know to have a complete game—the lofted pitch, the basic bunker shot, and the lag putt. If you can master these three shots, you're going to be able to escape at least 75 percent of the short game situations you find yourself in.

But what about the other 25 percent? In Chapter 4, we'll talk about the three hardest short game shots in golf—the pitch from deep grass close to the hole, the long bunker shot, and the awkward-distance pitch—and how you can get rid of your fear of them. You might not get up and down every time, even the pros don't in those situations. But you'll do a lot less damage to your score.

Once you have the shots you need, you need to know when to use them. In Chapter 5, we'll talk about basic short game strategy—how to "see" the hole and pick shots from your arsenal, and how things like lie and elevation dictate your choices. Chapter 6 provides you with the best strategies for deciphering bunker and trouble shots, while Chapter 7 is your complete guide to putting strategy. You probably aren't surprised to know that there's a lot more to successful putting than just lining it up and hoping it goes in. We'll talk about green reading, grain, wind, and other tour-caliber tricks to making the important ones.

In Chapter 8, I'll take you through some of the scoring lessons I've given tour players like Sergio Garcia. I'll show you how the process for elite athletes is a lot like it is for you, and some of the subtle ways it's different. And in Chapter 9, we'll take a tour of the shotmaker's bag—the equipment you need to practice your newfound art. I'll show you how to use the latest technological advancements to improve your stroke, and I'll help you understand how the makeup of your set changes based on the kinds of shots you're going to need on the courses you play.

THE ART OF

SCORING

Chapter 1

HOW LOW CAN YOU SCORE WITH THE SWING YOU HAVE?

· ·

What does it mean to have a good short game?

Before you answer, let me tell you that it's not quite as obvious as you think.

A player with a good short game certainly understands technique—things like having a good grip and setup, and an idea about how to swing the club. And good technique is part of it, but that's leaving out a really big piece.

Good short game players know how to look at a situation and see the best shot to hit.

If I had to break down the elements that have made players like Seve Ballesteros and Gary Player such short game geniuses, I'd put more weight on their ability to see *what* shot to hit than I would on their ability to understand the mechanics of *how* to hit it.

You're probably thinking to yourself, "That's fine if you're talking about a player who has world-class talent. But what about me? Don't I need to know *how* to hit the shots to get better?"

The reality is, most players have their priorities reversed. When they walk up to a shot from just off the green, or even set up for a putt, they don't really analyze the situation in front of them—or they drastically under-analyze it. Once they skip that pre-shot analysis, they click into overload mode and think about every piece of mechanical information they know about how to hit a shot that probably isn't even the right one for the situation at hand. It's no surprise, then, that 15-handicappers don't get up and down even 20 percent of the time, while PGA Tour players do it almost 70 percent of the time.

I'm not discounting the importance of technique. By the time you finish this book, you're going to have better short game mechanics. I'm going to show you how to hit six important shots— three basic ones and three difficult ones—in Chapters 3 and 4.

But to score consistently, you need to know more than technique. I'm going to show you how to see the options around and on the green, pick the right one, and then make your technique match the shot you see in your head. You're going to start hitting shots with intent—and that's what really separates poor short game players from good ones.

The best part about this process is that you're going to get remarkably better around the greens before you make any changes to your technique. Because picking the right shot—the shot that gives you the most chance of success with the least amount of risk—is more than half the battle.

How many times have you set up over a pitch or a bunker shot with a thought process that went something like, "I just hope I hit this up there somewhere close?" If you don't see a particular kind of shot—and where you want the ball to land, and how much you want it to roll—you're robbing yourself of all your best instincts. For example, if you're hitting a bunker shot, and you're focusing on the hole—not where you want the shot to land—your brain is going to send some mixed messages to your muscles. You're probably going to take a backswing that's too big for the shot, then decelerate the club on the downswing when you subconsciously realize you're going to hit the shot too far. And all of this happens independently of whether or not you actually know how to hit a basic bunker shot.

With a little bit of direction and some experience, you can become a much better short game player before you change a thing about your swing. To show you how this can happen in as little as three hours, I went out and played nine holes with three average-handicap players on the Judge course at Robert Trent Jones Golf Trail during a corporate engagement at the Navistar LPGA Classic in Prattville, Alabama.

I watched the three players—two 10-handicappers and a 19-handicapper—hit their short game shots, then I gave them advice about the shot they should have played. Some of it was related to their technique—a suggested swing thought, or a small adjustment in a grip or a stance. But the greatest changes came when I simply pointed out a better strategy. You'll be astonished at the difference in scoring my strategy advice made for these three guys—and how much of a difference it will make for you.

Scotty Aaron Webb is a 10-handicapper from Jasper, Alabama, and a former Division II college golfer. He's like a lot of better-than-average players in that he doesn't have what I'd call good fundamentals, but he plays a lot. Working with that kind of player is tricky, because the last thing I want to do is take away a shot that a player is comfortable with—even if my idea for what he should do is different. Scotty stood really close to the ball, with an open stance, so he couldn't help but take the club back in a very steep, up-and-down plane. As a result, he was great on low, running shots where he could close the face and put some hook spin on it. His challenge was finding a way to play soft, high shots, either from the rough or from the bunker.

John Primiano, the 19-handicapper from Tampa, is a powerful guy with a really bad grip. His right hand was so far under the handle that he couldn't do much but stab at the ground when it came time to hit a soft pitch. With a grip change, he could transform his whole game, but even before that, he got way better at just approaching each putt with a purpose instead of with a vague idea of getting it up by the hole.

Joey King is also from Jasper, Alabama, and like Scotty, he's a 10-handicapper. Where Scotty was more of a feel player, Joey was a guy who hadn't been playing his whole life but had gotten a lot of good instruction. His fundamentals were strong, but he really looked like a guy who was concentrating on setting the club in positions, instead of letting it go where it needed to go. For example, on his putting stroke, he was concentrating so hard on the mechanics that he took it back super slow, with stiff wrists and shoulder joints. I wanted him to learn to be more reactive and instinctive, rather than analytical.

Let's go through some of the scenarios we faced during that nine-hole stretch—situations that every golfer will be able to recognize—to show you what I mean.

HOLE NO. 1
Par 4, 400 yards

We all hit good shots from the elevated tee box, fifty feet above the wide fairway. John hit his second shot into a big fairway bunker 40 yards short of the green and had an awkward shot in. He tried to hit a big explosion shot, but topped it and left it in the bunker. For the second shot, I told him to think of it as more of a punch chip, and forget about the fact that he was in the sand. Many players just automatically default to an open-the-stance-and-hit-behind-it bunker shot for anything that isn't a full swing, and that's just not the right shot a lot of the time. For John's shot, the feel is that you're hitting a thin shot, with not too much swing. If you do catch the ball thin, you don't need as much clubhead speed to shoot it out of the bunker.

(ABOVE LEFT) John had a long bunker shot, and he tried to play it like a big explosion shot, hitting behind the ball and using the bounce to splash it out.

(ABOVE RIGHT) From longer than 25 or 30 yards, you need to play more of a punch chip shot from sand, assuming you don't have a tall lip in your way.

He hit his second shot pretty well, up onto the fringe, but he left his fifty-footer from there way short. He needed to keep in mind that on a fringe putt from short, manicured grass, the length of the fringe isn't going to have much effect on the ball. He needed to take a bigger backswing to account for the longer shot. The tendency is to make a short backswing and power the club through faster. That's a recipe for inconsistent contact.

NO. 2
Par 4,371 yards

This hole curves to the right, and the fairway tilts right to throw sliced tee shots down into a thickly grassed area with lots of awkward sidehill lies. Joey hit a good tee shot, but missed the green right and short. He had a short pitch from a sidehill lie, with the ball below his feet. The conventional wisdom for full shots is that sidehill lies with the ball below your feet are going to produce left-to-right shots. That might be true, but on pitches, you'll actually have a tendency to pull those shots left. You have to be aware of that, and either account for it or keep more control of the club-face through impact.

When Joey hit his shot, the heel caught and he pulled it, hitting it long and off the left side of the green. When he hit a second ball, I asked him to simply aim a little bit more right to account for the heel catching, and open the face of his wedge a little at address. The bounce on the club glided more easily through the grass, and he hit it in the middle of the green.

(ABOVE LEFT) From a sidehill lie in the rough, Joey had the ball below his feet. He adjusted his aim to the left, because he thought the ball was going to slice.

(ABOVE RIGHT) But from that kind of sidehill lie, the heel of the club has a tendency to grab in the grass, which causes the face to close and shoot the ball left. That's why Joey's ball went long and left.

NO. 3
Par 3,155 yards

From the tee box, you can see three distinct tiers on this green and a collection area to the left. With the pin on the front left tier, it's a much easier second shot if you're either on the same tier as the flag, or chipping from that tier. Scotty hit his tee shot onto the green, but to the wrong tier, leaving himself with a putt that was harder than a basic chip from around the correct tier would have been. He had to read the difference in slope and the strong grain that was coming toward him, and he left the chip way short and on the wrong tier, then three-putted. I had him recalibrate the landing point for his chip so that it was up much closer to the hole. That way, if he hit it a little too far, he'd still be on the correct tier and in reasonable two-putt range.

NO. 4
Par 5, 514 yards

With a good tee shot on this risk-reward par 5, you have a chance to hit a 5-wood onto the green. But if you decide to do that, and you don't hit the green, it's clear that you want to miss it long and left, in a fringe-cut chipping area. Short and left is in a pond, and short right is in a big, deep bunker. Scotty played his second shot just right, bouncing it onto the green and long, into the chipping area. He actually got kind of unlucky in that it hung up on a downhill lie. He played a delicate chip, from tight rough to a downhill pin, down to tap-in range—a great shot. If that's a shot he's comfortable hitting, I don't have a problem with it, especially given the results. But from a downhill lie, to a close pin that's also on a downhill, I'd tell even a tour player to putt that one. You've got a lot more room to make a mistake and not get penalized too greatly. Catch that delicate chip a little bit thin, and it's down the hill and gone.

NO. 5
Par 4,386 yards

On this straightforward par 4, Joey hit a great tee shot right down the middle and had a short iron into the hole. He hit it to twenty feet, straight up the hill and into the grain. But on his birdie putt, he made the same mistake a lot of amateur players make when they're presented with the chance to do something exciting—and a birdie putt is exciting. Instead of letting the clubhead swing, he made a mechanical, overcontrolled stroke. He didn't hit the putt squarely and didn't give it enough energy. It ended up about a foot short.

There's a very strong connection between your vision and the way your brain makes your muscles move. No matter what kind of putting stroke you have, you're going to get your best results if you make your read and focus on your target while standing square to it—looking with both eyes—and hitting the putt as soon as possible. The more you wait, the more you compromise your talent. Watching Joey stand over his putt, I could almost see all of his mechanical thoughts in a big thought-bubble. And as the seconds ticked by, you could see the touch and feel flow out of him. The only thing left was mechanical.

NO. 6
Par 3,190 yards

This is a long, tough hole, with water all around the front of the green and a steep, grassy slope long and left. Joey hit his shot to the flat on the other side of that grassy slope, which left him with a flop shot high over the hill to a tight pin. He had the technique under control, but he didn't pay close enough attention to the grain on the green around where his shot had to land. The green looked dark, like carpeting that's been pulled toward you. That meant he was going into the grain, which would kill off any roll he had on the shot. Sure enough, he hit a nice shot, but it stopped dead, and he two-putted for bogey.

If the darkness or shininess of the grass isn't obvious, you can always look at the cup to see which way the grain is growing, too. If the grain is growing from left to right, the left edge of the cup will be clean, while the right edge will be ripped up.

You can check the direction of the grain on the green in two ways. If the grass looks shinier from one direction, you're looking down grain. Another way is to check the hole. The edge of the cup will be torn up in the direction the grain is moving.

NO. 7
Par 5,586 yards

A three-shot hole for virtually every player, this hole is more about the strategy of the second-shot layup. John hit a good tee shot, but it trickled into a fairway bunker. He then hit a good hybrid shot out of the bunker into the middle of the fairway, 150 yards out, to get back into position. The key to saving shots on long holes is to pick out the worst place around the green to be, then do everything you can to stay away from it. On No. 7, the deep bunker short and right was that bad place to be. Unfortunately, it's right where John went, too, and he had a long bunker shot to a tier on the back of the green.

He misread the tier and the grain, and left the bunker shot on the bottom tier. Three putts. On a long bunker shot, the tendency is to want to swing fast. A better swing thought is to swing big—more backswing, with a complete pivot—instead of thinking about lots of speed at the bottom.

Scotty's approach shot ended up just short of the green, and he had the same tier to deal with that John did. He had three options, to pitch the ball up on top of the tier, chip it and let it run up the hill, or putt it. He chose to putt, which was a good move because he was heavy into the grain—which has a tendency to catch the club if you're using a wedge. But Scotty didn't give his putt enough power to offset the effect of the grain, and he didn't get the ball back to the right tier.

Scotty picked the right shot from the fringe—a putt from grain that was heavy into him—but he didn't give the putt enough speed to reach the same tier as the flag.

NO. 8
Par 4, 420 yards

So how do you figure out where to miss? It's a lot like playing pool. You're thinking two shots ahead, not just one. John blocked his tee shot right, behind some trees and in line with deep bunkers on the right and short. He pitched successfully through the trees, but had a tough second pitch to a short pin right over those big bunkers. He changed his spine angle on the pitch and stood up on it. He caught it thin and hit it over the green, where he had a difficult little pitch shot that required him to swing into strong grain where his ball was sitting. From there, it took him three to get down.

When you're looking at a shot where the club will have to travel through wiry grass growing right at you, you have to be very cautious. You have to keep turning and swinging through. If you quit on it at all, the club will get snarled in the grass and you'll dump the shot short.

NO. 9
Par 4,387 yards

This hole is pretty straightforward, and it's uphill the entire way from tee to green. John left himself with a 40-yard pitch from an uphill lie, in front of the green, but he left it short of his target. That's very common on a shot like that, because the tilt of the ground adds to the effective loft of your club. You're shooting the ball even higher into the air—especially if you're scooping at it with your hands—and not putting enough pressure on the ball to make it go forward in addition to going up in the air.

John's ball rested on a little upslope, which added to the effective loft of his club. The tendency on these shots is to leave it short, and that's what he did here.

The result after the nine holes was that the 10-handicappers, Scotty and Joey, could have saved at least two or three shots— enough to cut three or four shots from their handicap in the near term—just by making strategy decisions on basic things like the safe places to miss, shot selection, and condition elements like lie and grain. John had a bigger handicap—and he's a good athlete—so there was even more room for improvement there. It wouldn't be crazy to suggest he could get five or six shots better right away. And we haven't even started talking about technique yet.

Now, some of that improvement is attributable to the fact that the three guys I played with had long games that were pretty good when compared to their short games. In the next chapter, I'm going to show you how to assess your own game and figure out where you can make the most improvement, both in terms of strategy and technique. And it *is* different for every player.

If I played in a shamble with a variety of different amateurs—a shamble is where the tour player hits a tee shot and everybody plays from that spot—playing from the fairway would help everybody. But it would help the guy whose 20-handicap came from hitting five tee shots out of play per round the most. He's the guy who makes a decent score because he has a pretty good short game.

But in my experience, the most common 20-handicapper is the guy who can advance the ball pretty well, but has trouble getting on the green and one-putting or even two-putting. He's been spending his entire golf career around the green hoping something good happens. He's not doing things intentionally, and he for sure doesn't think he has options.

I know that *any* player is going to improve by following the strategy and technique tips in this book, but that kind of 20-handicapper—the one who is hoping instead of doing things intentionally—is going to see a dramatic improvement.

Chapter 2

WHAT ARE YOUR SHORT GAME AND PUTTING HANDICAPS?

· ·

When somebody asks you for your handicap, you probably know what to say. You'll either give them your official index, like 12.3, or your course handicap, 14 or 15.

But we all know that an overall handicap number only tells part of the story when it comes to describing a person's golf game. It's just that—an overall handicap. You might have a vague idea that you're better with your driver and 3-wood than you are around the green, or that you prefer hitting short irons to standing over a ten-footer for par.

There's really no reason to be vague about it, though. Do you know where you're wasting shots, and what parts of your short game could use the most work?

By playing some practice rounds at your regular course and diligently recording the shots you hit, you can gain some tremendous insight into the specifics of both your short and long games. All it takes is a blank scorecard and a little practice walking off distances. Generally speaking, each step is three feet—which equals a yard. That will give you a rough estimate of how far your target is.

I'll take you through exactly how to determine your short game and putting "handicaps"—scores you can use alongside your official USGA handicap number to assess the state of your game. Better yet, you'll be able to see right away which parts of your game need work—both right now, before you read the rest of this book, and later, when you're doing checkup work during your season. You'll have a fantastic tool that you can use to make sure all the parts of your game are staying healthy and trending in the right direction.

When I'm watching a tour player or an amateur play out on the golf course, I'm essentially creating in my mind different scores for the way he or she handles short game shots and putting. A variety of factors go into that score. How is the player performing relative to his or her ability level? Is he or she using a specific kind of strategy for shots, or just hitting and hoping? What kind of athlete are we talking about? We all have talent. Some people just have more of it. How much learning about golf has he or she done? Is the technique that's being used happening on purpose?

Take a 15-handicapper in a common short game situation, for example. Let's say the pin is back right, he's in front of the green on the left, and there's a tier with a break to the back right. Let's say he just walks up and takes his sand wedge and swings away. That tells me he didn't pick a place to land his shot, and he didn't think about what trajectory he wanted to hit it. I see people all the time who just walk into the bunker and try to whack the ball out without thinking about anything else—not where they want the ball to land, or what it will do after that.

On the other hand, if I see a guy walk up and look at the slope and pace off the distance, it's almost like I can see his mind processing the shot. Maybe he's pulling out an 8-iron and deciding where to land it. That shows that he's established an intent for the shot, which is the first step.

Step two is, if there is a plan for the shot, is it a good one? Does it match the player's skill set? I was playing with my friend Tom, and he hit a shot four feet over the back edge of the green, into a lie where the ball was sitting down in Bermuda rough. It wasn't going to be easy to get the clubhead on the ball, and he only had about twenty feet of green to work with. I watched him get in there and try to lift the ball out of that grass with his sand wedge, and he skulled it over the green and into the hazard. He saw a shot and a strategy, but he didn't pick the one that matched his skill set. Maybe the right shot to hit was a hybrid with a putt swing, just to the edge of the putting surface. It might have dribbled ten feet on, leaving him with a putt. At the minimum, he would have advanced the ball out of trouble without a lot of risk.

After the strategy decision is done, you have to watch what the ball is doing. That might sound simple, but a lot of players—and teachers—get hoodwinked into making unnecessary technique changes. If a player is really making the ball do what he or she wants it to do—even if it isn't with a method I'd suggest—I don't know that I'd be anxious to make a lot of changes. There are a lot of guys with funky shooting mechanics making a lot of money in the NBA. My goal is always to get a player to see more available shots and make that player better at getting the ball to go where he wants it to go.

A ton of average amateur players come off the course feeling like they've wasted a lot of short game shots. That's a normal feeling, especially if you don't get a chance to practice very much. My goal here is to help you understand exactly what you do versus what you could reasonably expect from yourself given your talent level—and the difficulty of the shot you're facing—so you know when to be upset about a mental error and when to give yourself a break because you just had a hard shot.

Expectations are obviously different for players of different overall handicap levels, so I'm going to break down some goals and strategies for a variety of playing levels. And those playing levels hold true for the various elements of the short game and putting, too. You might be a scratch amateur player, but a really mediocre sand player. If you're realistic about your skill level, you know where you stand and have a better idea of what you need to do to get better. And you're going to be happier about hitting a 20-yard greenside bunker shot to ten feet than a tour player would be. Or at least you should be.

Another thing I'm going to show you is how all the various measurements of the short game and putting—and even the long game—are related to each other. You can set for yourself a goal of averaging thirty putts per round or less, but you have to understand that that statistic is directly related to the number of greens you hit, and how well you hit your short game shots. If you hit a lot of greens with longer clubs, you're going to take more putts just because you're in position to do so more often.

In my own PGA Tour career, I know there have been seasons when my putting stats looked fantastic because I was hitting my short game shots so well. I had a lot of tap-ins. And the numbers that a tour player looks at might not be directly applicable to you, but the overall principles are the same. A tour player who hits fourteen greens might be happy with thirty-one putts per round. You might be happy with thirty-five. A tour player needs to know how many putts from inside thirty feet he's leaving three feet or less from the hole. You need to know how many you're leaving within five feet. We can all be practicing certain things to make our numbers get smaller. Then, if both your short game and your putting are improving, you're trimming from both ends of the string.

When I played tour events, I created a system of filling out my scorecard that was more than simply the number of strokes I took for a particular hole. On the next page are the cards I filled out for a tournament I played in 1999 on the Nike Tour (and where I lost in a playoff to Curt Byrum).

In the top left of the score box, I marked an X if I hit the fairway. In the bottom left, I marked another X if I hit the green. The number on the top right is how many putts I took, and the number on the bottom right is how many of the total shots I took on the hole I made while completely committed—with no negative thoughts. For example, if I said to myself, "Don't hit it to the right" before the shot, I didn't get credit for being fully committed and positive—even if the result of the shot was OK. Keeping that tally really makes you stay on task in terms of concentrating and giving your best effort on every swing. If Jay Haas wins the season-long Charles Schwab Cup by a few points, it might be because of a single shot he hit at a single tournament during the year—a shot he was fully committed to hitting. And that's the difference between collecting $1 million or nothing. I can honestly say that I paid closer attention to that commitment number than I did to the actual score I shot, because the commitment number was something totally under my control, while my score could have been affected by good or bad bounces.

Nike South FL. 1999 #①

Hole	1	②	3	④	5	6	7	8	9	Out		10	11	⑫	13	14	⑮	16	⑰	18	In	Total
My Score	5	3	5	2	5	3	4	4	4	35		4	5	2	4	4	3	3	4	4	33	

Nike South FL R②

Hole	1	2	3	4	5	6	7	8	9	Out		10	11	12	⑬	14	15	16	⑰	18	In	Total
My Score	4	4	4	3	5	3	4	4	4			4	6	3	3	4	4	3	4	4		

D-jason   N-South FL R③

Hole	①	②	3	4	5	⑥	⑦	8	9	Out		10	11	12	13	14	15	16	17	⑱	In	Total
My Score	2	3	4	3	5	2	3	4	4			4	5	4	4	4	4	3	5	3		

Nike South FL R④

Hole	①	②	③	4	⑤	6	7	8	9	Out		10	11	12	13	14	15	16	17	18	In	Total
My Score	3	3	3	4	4	3	4	5	4			4	5	3	4	5	4	3	6	4		

When I played in tour events, I'd fill out the bottom of my scorecard with different notations that recorded more than just the score I made on each hole. In each box, I put an X in the top left corner if I hit the fairway, another X in the bottom left if I hit the green, the number of putts I took in the top right corner, and the number of shots on the hole I hit while I was totally committed to my target.

....

WHAT DOES THIS MEAN FOR YOU?

You can keep some simple-to-record statistics on your own short game to get a much clearer picture of what you actually do around and on the greens.

The next time you go out to play a practice round, take a friend who's as interested as you are in breaking down some short game stats. Start by measuring how far away you are from the hole on every full-swing approach shot you hit. In other words, if you're aiming for the green with your full shot, make a note of how far away you were on each one. What you're getting here is a stark assessment of just how good—or bad—you are at hitting your target on an approach shot. Then, make a notation about where the shot ended up—on the green (G), in the rough (R), on the fringe (F), in a bunker (B), or out of play (O).

The next step is to measure the distance you have from the hole after hitting each short game shot from 30 yards off the green or closer. When you look at this total, you'll get a strong sense of two things—how good your chipping, pitching, and sand game is, and how difficult the short game shots you're leaving yourself are.

Then, when you get on the green, count the number of total putts you've taken. As I said earlier, this number is hugely dependent on how close you're hitting the ball to the hole on both approach shots and short game shots, but it's still a good barometer—especially if you track it with the next barometer. Once you make your first putt, measure how far away you are from the cup. If you have a tap-in, call it one foot. From that measurement, you can determine both an average second-putt length and the total feet of putts you have.

Now, you have four sets of figures you can track, just like you would a USGA handicap. And no matter what your numbers say, they're relative to your specific level of play. That means you can be just as pleased about improving your second putt distance from twelve feet to eight as you can bumping it down from four feet to three.

These pure measurement stats are just one piece of the puzzle. The next thing I want you to track is the relative difficulty of each short game shot you have to hit, and your own assessment of how well you execute the shot.

I use a straightforward grading system that is calibrated for players at different overall handicap levels. Start with every short game shot around the green. For an easy shot—meaning a standard pitch or chip with lots of green to work with, or a basic bunker shot—call it an "A." For a medium-difficulty shot—involving some rough, or a sketchy lie—call it a "B." For a very difficult shot—buried in the bunker, deep grass, extreme sidehill lie—call it a "C." If you hit it into the hazard or somewhere else unplayable, call it a "D."

Now you can grade yourself on the outcome of each shot from the different levels of difficulty, relative to your overall handicap.

Result from "A" Shot
Scratch–10 handicap: Within three feet
11–20 handicap: Within eight feet
Over 20 handicap: Within fifteen feet

Result from "B" Shot
Scratch–10 handicap: Within eight feet
11–20 handicap: Within fifteen feet
Over 20 handicap: Within thirty feet

Result from "C" Shot
Scratch–10 handicap: Within twenty feet
11–20 handicap: Within thirty feet
Over 20 handicap: Out of trouble

Performing this exercise does two important things. One, it forces you to make an assessment of each shot you hit, so you're thinking very concretely about your short game. Second, it gives you a much more accurate frame of reference about "success" versus "failure." A tour player knows that on a very difficult downhill lie pitch to a tight pin, a shot that ends up twenty feet from the hole might be a fantastic result. That's a "success." On the other side of the coin, a straightforward chip up the hill to an easy flag is a "failure" if it settles six feet from the flag. You develop a much better way to peg your expectations to the shot at hand—and your level of proficiency on a certain kind of shot.

You can also drill down one more level by keeping track of each kind of short game shot you face, in general categories. Then you'll have a record of the difficulty of the shot, plus whether you passed or failed when trying to execute it.

The important categories (which we're going to break down later in the book) are greenside bunker shots, standard pitches and chips, long pitches, long bunker shots, trouble shots and long putts (over thirty feet).

Before we talk more about putting, I want to go over some of the general questions you should be asking yourself about your short game as you go through this process.

Scratch–10 handicap

- Did you have a definite plan on every short game shot?
- Given the situation, did you balance the probability of hitting it close versus the risk of hitting a shot that puts you in even more trouble? Even tour players tend to play more conservatively in the short game

to avoid really bad shots. For example, Phil Mickelson picks very difficult shots—like a lob off a tight lie to a tight pin—more often, but he gets away with it because he's so talented, and because he can often recover and save bogey. A marginally less-talented tour player could try the same shot but make a double bogey two or three times more out of ten tries. That might mean a missed cut.

10–20 handicap

- Did you have a definite plan on every short game shot?
- Did you pick a shot that was realistic given your skill set?
- Are there short game shots you try to avoid as you play a round? Why?
- If so, did you pick a strategy that suited that decision? For example, most 10- and over handicappers really struggle with 50- and 60-yard pitch shots. Basically, they put a full arm swing on a half shot. But they do nothing to avoid hitting that shot. If they're 240 in, they take as much club as they can and try to get as close to the green as possible. From 240 yards out, even if they were able to hit a decent 3-wood—say, 85 percent of max distance—they would end up with a 50-yard pitch. In other words, a pretty good play puts the player in position to hit a shot he hates. The much better play—on both shots—is to hit a shorter, straighter layup, and a shorter iron with a full swing into the green.

20 and over handicap

- How many situations do you find yourself in where you feel like you don't have any short game shot you can confidently hit to get to the middle of the green?
- How often does it take you two (or more) short game shots to get on the green?

Once you get on the green, you're going to go through a similar process in terms of pegging your results to the difficulty of the shot you faced. When I'm teaching a tour player, the most common complaint I get is that the ball isn't coming off the face with a chance to go in the hole. Tour players are realistic enough to know that they're going to make some and miss some, but when putts from thirty feet and in never have a chance to go in, that drives them crazy. Obviously, you're going to have your own set of expectations based on your overall handicap level—and how good a putter you are.

0–10 handicap

- Making solid contact is very important. At this level, you might pick the wrong speed or the wrong line, but keep track of how many times you hit the ball solidly, in the middle of the putterface. The more times you hit the ball solidly with the putter, the better you'll dial in your distance control.
- Be aware of where you leave your next putt, especially from thirty feet and in. You can go through the same grading system you used for the results of your short

game shots—A for three feet or less, B for three to six feet, C for ten to twenty feet and D for more than twenty feet.

- Measure the total number of feet of putts you make. This gives you an interesting read on what parts of your game are working on a given day—and to what you can attribute a good or bad round. For example, if you shoot a career best score and make one hundred feet of putts, you can be fairly sure you posted that score because you made some long putts. You can certainly improve your putting and have a better chance of hitting long putts close, but making a bunch of them in one round is more about luck than skill—and something you can't count on doing over and over. The opposite point is true, as well. Maybe you weren't thrilled with your score, but you see that you only made forty feet of putts. That indicates you hit the ball much better than you scored. Again, you can improve your overall stroke, but some days, the ball just doesn't go in. You're getting a much more accurate read on your game, and on what your expectations should be.

11 and over handicap

- Here's where higher-handicap players can make a dramatic improvement right away—to the point where there's no major difference between a 22-handicapper's putting skill and an 11-handicapper's.
- You need to be more lenient with yourself than the player in the previous grouping, but you should still

measure how many times you hit it solid. Your real goal is three-putt avoidance. You're trying to be in good shape to make the next one, even if you're six feet away.

- How many times did a putt break the opposite way from what you expected? You're measuring your capacity to read putts correctly. A small improvement in that skill can slice off significant distance in the putts you leave yourself. For example, if you read a thirty-foot putt to have three feet of break to the right, but it actually breaks one foot left, you can hit the putt at perfect speed and still have four feet left. If you improve your read slightly—just to the point where you see a hint of break to the left, you're leaving yourself a one- or two-footer instead. Tour players make two-footers 99 percent of the time. They make four-footers 75 percent of the time. It's probably safe to say the spread is greater for the average amateur— and enough to make a huge difference in your score.

All of this might sound like a lot of work, but if you play just two or three practice rounds with a friend (you can help each other step off the measurements) and record this data, you're going to have a treasure trove of information. The definition of what you do on the golf course is going to go from a hunch or a guess to a concrete measure of your tendencies. And I'll bet that no matter what your level of play, you'll be surprised by some of the results.

You're also going to be able to take that information and use it to apply the strategy and technique tips throughout this book in the most effective way.

Chapter 3

THE THREE BASIC SHOTS YOU NEED TO KNOW TODAY

· ·

One big misconception that a lot of players come in with is the idea that they have to master a whole bunch of new shots before they can make a big dent in their handicap.

That's just not true.

Will you shoot better scores if you learn how to hit a variety of different shots? Of course. But the most common short game situations you're going to face around and on the green are pretty straightforward. In other words, most of these situations will call for one of the three most basic shots: a standard pitch, a bunker shot, or a putt.

How well you execute "vanilla" shots like these goes a long way toward determining your score for the day. If you consistently mis-hit basic pitch and chip shots, and you have no idea how to roll your thirty- and forty-footers within a reasonable range of the cup, you won't break any scoring goals—like breaking 100, 80, or even winning a PGA Tour event.

That's right. Even tour players overlook the importance of the basic shots. Some of the most dramatic success stories I've been a part of as a teacher have involved tour players who have gotten up and down more often with straightforward pitches, basic sand shots that end up closer to the hole, and an improved putting stroke. Sergio Garcia is a prime example of a tour player who struggled with these shots (and I'll talk more about what we did to improve them in Chapter 8).

When I share this with the students who come to see me at a one-day clinic, they're sometimes a little bit surprised that the short game "answer" isn't more complicated. But just think about the last round you played. You probably had some funky lies, or a time when you had to hit something low under a tree branch, or you needed to flop a shot high over a bunker. But no matter what scores you shoot, I guarantee you had at least thirty shots that fall into the category of basic pitch shots, greenside bunker shots and putts of thirty feet or more. There's more room to improve your score by improving your technique on these three basic shots because there are so many more opportunities to use these shots in every round.

In the next chapter, I'll show you how to avoid the double- and triple-bogeys that come from making mistakes on super-hard short game shots like ones from the bunker 40 yards away. But if you can improve on these three basic ones, you can make a significant change in your handicap—in a weekend. How significant? A 20-handicapper could cut five shots. And that's without making any changes in his or her full swing.

THE BASIC PITCH

When I give a one-day clinic, the first shot I teach is the basic pitch shot, because it's easily the most versatile short game shot you can have. You can hit it from almost any lie, because when you do it right, you don't have to be precise about where you hit the ground. The bounce on the bottom of the club—the slab of metal that protrudes from the sole—skips along the ground. Even if you hit an inch or two behind the ball, the shot will get up in the air and land fairly softly, without a lot of backspin. That makes it a very predictable shot, and predictable is the name of the game when it comes to greenside shots.

On a pitch shot, the average amateur's tendency is to want to try to lift the ball in the air—by leaning back, away from the target, and either by using the right hand to scoop at the ball, or by physically tugging up and toward the target with the grip end of the club.

All three of these mistakes make it difficult for you to find a consistent bottom to your swing. When your swing is reaching its low point in a different place every time, you're going to hit a lot of fat and thin shots. One other factor that I often see giving players a hard time is a too-strong grip—particularly when the right hand is turned to the right and under the shaft. With a strong grip, you'll bring the clubface back pointed at the ground (closed), and the leading edge will dig into the ground on the way through impact.

If I lost you right there, don't worry too much. Let's start from the beginning. One of the fundamental things I teach is that— with the exception of some super-high-lofted specialty shots— the basics of every short game shot are the same. When it comes to grip, stance, and setup, if you're in what I call a solid, neutral position, you are giving yourself the best chance to make solid contact.

It all starts with a good grip. I play every shot around the green with my normal grip—the same one I use to hit a driver or a 5-iron.

To find your grip, start by standing tall with your arms relaxed at your sides. Now look down at your left hand and notice the position it's in. I find most of my students' hands will turn in slightly, so that the back of the left hand is at a 45-degree angle, instead of lying parallel to the left leg. From this position, place the grip of the club in the fingers of your left hand—along the creases created by the first knuckles. After you get it in the fingers, squeeze down the palm of your left hand on the grip. The left thumb should be slightly right of center when you look down on the top of the grip.

Next, wrap the fingers of your right hand onto the grip, and connect the lifeline of your right hand to the side of your left thumb. You are overlapping your right pinkie finger and left index finger. You should sense the grip down in the fingers, and your wrists should feel very mobile and soft as you waggle the club in front of you.

Why is it so important for the grip to be in the fingers? Take a wadded up piece of paper in your hand and throw it underhand into the trash can. Now, did you balance the paper in your palm and toss it that way, or did you hold the paper in your fingertips? If you balanced the paper on your palm, you probably missed the basket.

Once you have the club in your fingers, check to see if your grip is weak, neutral, or strong. I'm sure you've heard those terms thrown around in golf instruction, but let me give you my definition, so we're all on the same page. If you set your grip and hold it up in front of your chest, the V's created by the sides of your hands and your thumbs will point to your right collarbone in a neutral grip. In a weak grip, the V's point almost straight up, toward your chin. In a strong grip, the V's turn more to the right, so that they're aimed at your right shoulder. (Remember to reverse all of these directions if you're a left-hander.) You can also have your hands independently turned to different degrees of weak and strong. For example, if you turned your left hand farther left on the grip, toward the target, and your right hand farther right on the grip, away from the target, your left hand would be set up really weak, and your right would be really strong.

Here's another way to check your grip. Take your grip and stand up tall. Raise and lower the shaft straight up and down in front of you, using only your wrists as the lever. When you have the club hinged in the upright position, the clubface will remain vertical if you have your hands in the neutral position. If the toe of the club leans left, your grip is too strong. If it leans to the right, your grip is too weak. I'm always looking to share a perfect grip with my students, but if you have to make a mistake in one direction, I prefer a grip that's a little too strong to one that is too weak. It's easier to pinch the ball than it is to scoop it.

The reason I'm going over the grip in such detail is because I want you to be able to use your hands and wrists for feel, not take them completely out of play for short shots. I also want you to be able to start to identify your good and bad shots based on how the ball reacts when you hit it. For example, if your grip is too weak, you'll probably feel more comfortable hitting high shots, although they'll probably come up short and right a lot. You will also struggle when you want to play a shot with a lower trajectory. If your grip is too strong, you'll play most of your shots with a driving trajectory, sometimes pulled to the left, and feel very uncomfortable when you have to play a high shot or a bunker shot. You will also tend to take a deep divot, or even have the leading edge get stuck in the ground at impact because the club is coming into the ball delofted and on such a steep angle.

One other thing to remember about your grip is that it isn't something you can just set and forget. If you don't pay regular attention to it, it can drift weak or strong and cause inconsistencies to creep into your short game. I teach tour players who hit thousands of pitch and chip shots every week, and a lot of the time I spend with them out at tournaments is devoted to giving checkups to make sure fundamentals like the grip haven't drifted out of whack. And I really have to keep after students who have

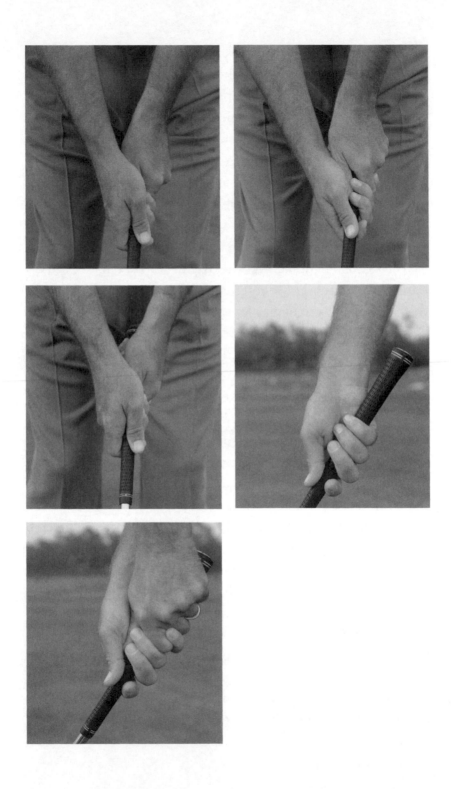

(ABOVE LEFT) With the hands in a neutral grip, the V's created between my thumbs and the sides of my hands point toward my right collarbone. The grip lets my hands and wrists release correctly in the shot.

(ABOVE RIGHT) When the hands rotate away from the target into a strong position like this, you reduce the effective loft of the club and the leading edge tends to dig into the ground. Notice how the V's point to my right shoulder.

(MIDDLE LEFT) When the hands rotate toward the target into a weak position, the V's point straight up, toward my chin. With a weak grip, you'll tend to hit a lot of shots high, short, and to the right.

(MIDDLE RIGHT) For pitch shots the grip is identical to the one you would use on your full shots. You can see the grip is down in the fingers, so that the shaft runs along the crease where your first knuckle attaches to your palm.

(BELOW LEFT) On a good pitch shot, the wrists hinge and release. This is why the club should rest in the fingers and sit at an angle to the forearms. Compare this to the putting grip later in this chapter, where the shaft is in line with the forearms.

....

made a grip change to stay committed to the change, instead of going back to what is comfortable.

For the basic pitch—and almost every other non-sand shot around the green—your stance and posture are going to stay fairly consistent. The first goal is to get into a position that will let you hit shots without tension and stiffness. If you get yourself into a rigid position, with your arms locked or the muscles in your legs tensed up, you're never going to have a good short game. Watch an athlete performing a "touch" maneuver like shooting a free throw or a concert pianist at the keyboard and you won't see anything stiff or mechanical. All the moves are fluid and graceful. I want you to develop that same sense of fluidity and feel in your short game.

(ABOVE LEFT) When you set up for a pitch shot, your arms should be soft and relaxed—they should hang from your shoulders, so you don't have to stretch for the ball.

(ABOVE RIGHT) If you extend your arms and tighten your muscles at address, you rob yourself of touch and feel, and you'll have a tendency to move the handle too much instead of swinging the clubhead back on plane.

For greenside shots, I narrow my stance, which makes it easy to rotate my lower body instead of rocking or swaying. I don't want you to feel like your lower body is encased in concrete. You need to make a pivot (not a sway) and a narrower stance helps that. What's the difference between a pivot and a sway? A sway is when the hips slide straight back away from the target, as if you were trying to get out of the way of getting tagged in touch football. In a pivot, the hips *turn* instead of shift back, as they would if you were tossing something underhanded.

In terms of aiming my body, I set up square to the target

line or even slightly closed to it. In other words, if you held a shaft on my shoulders and another one on my hips, both shafts would point parallel to the target line (the line between the ball and where I want the ball to go), or slightly to the right of it. Many, many players are taught to set up open with the shoulders, hips or both (so that the shafts would point to the left of

(ABOVE LEFT) For a pitch shot, your stance is similar to the one you'd use for a short-iron shot: the shoulders, hips, and feet are square to the target line, the ball is just ahead of the middle of the stance, and the shaft is not leaned forward, toward the target. Two thirds of my weight is on my front foot, and it will stay there through the swing.

(ABOVE MIDDLE) Many players are taught to hit short game shots with the ball far back in an open stance. I think this makes the shot much more complicated than it has to be.

(ABOVE RIGHT) If I'm hitting a shorter shot, my stance gets narrower and my hands move slightly more ahead of the ball, toward the target. On this shot, I'm hitting the ball first, then the grass.

the target). I want to aim everything down the line I want my ball to travel on.

On most of my short shots, my weight starts out 65 to 70 percent on my left side, and that balance doesn't change throughout the swing. My idea of how to keep the weight left seems radical to some students. The first step is to keep the upper spine tilted slightly left—toward the target. One way to feel this is to bend straight over, then slide your hips to the right. The left shoulder will then seem to be lower than the right shoulder. In order to hold the club and hit a shot, your left arm will then be bent more than your right from this position.

If I'm teaching you and I get you with your weight favoring the left in this manner, I'll bet you're going to tell me it feels like 90 percent of your weight is left. But that's only because so many players think that keeping the weight to the left means sliding the hips towards the target—which tilts the spine back and causes fat and thin shots.

That tilt to the right is by far the most common mistake I see in the setup, and it has the most damaging consequences. When your right shoulder is lower than your left, it *feels* like that would help you get more loft on your shots, but it really just makes it easier for you to blade it or dig the club into the ground a couple of inches behind the ball, especially if you're making common mistake number two, which is playing the ball too far back in your stance. People are typically taught to hit the ball with a descending blow, and it would seem that moving the ball back in the stance would help you to hit it this way. It will help, but this is really doing it the hard way, and it makes it very difficult to make consistent contact. If you play the ball in the middle of your stance with your weight and tilt favoring your *left* instead of your right side, you're going to make that descending blow, but also get the benefit of the club's true loft.

I'm not in favor of taking an open stance to hit your chip or pitch shots, because it encourages you to take the club back outside the target line, away from your body. The only way to hit a good shot is to push or block the ball onto the target line. I think people have been told it's easier to turn through and be in a good impact position if you set up open. I understand those thoughts. But my short shots don't require a lot of follow-through. My club is done by the time it's two to three feet past the ball. I want to set up so that it's extremely easy to reach my backswing position, so I'm in a good position to start down. Just like putting, my backswing varies depending on how far I want to hit the shot, but my follow-through stays pretty similar, unless I need to hit a really high shot. By setting up square, it's so much easier to get the club into an on-plane position in the takeaway, where all I have to do is pivot through.

Although I see more players set up with the right shoulder low, the ball too far back and the stance open and aimed to the left in an open stance, I occasionally see players get the ball too far forward. This usually happens without them even knowing it. The cause of this problem is that the player has flared the left foot way open. When this happens, it's the foot that's causing the bad ball position. If you think this is your problem, here is your test: Take your setup, and then, without moving your left heel, turn the left toe perpendicular to the target line. The ball will usually be an inch or two in front of your left foot (toward the target), way out in front, and in a difficult spot to hit consistently with good contact. The middle of your stance is the center between your heels, not your toes. My left toe might be slightly open when I set up to a shot, but my toe line—the imaginary line you draw in front of your feet—is definitely parallel to the target line or pointing slightly to the right of it. The ball is inside my left heel.

Another common mistake I see players make is starting with the shaft leaning too far forward—toward the target. This usually happens because of a combination of other mistakes. If your ball position is too far back and your stance is open, you pretty much have to have your hands forward to be able to hit the ball without crashing the club into the ground six inches behind the ball. The concept of delofting the club is good—it helps you play shots by hitting the ball first, as opposed to the ground. But to me, it puts the player in the opposite position I like. It gets the body "shallow" and the club in a "steep" position. Let me stop for a second and tell you what I mean by those terms. The angle that your clubhead approaches the ball can be a sharp descending blow, or a more shallow sweeping motion. Two major factors in your clubhead descent to the ball are the position of your spine (from a face-on view) and the way you swing the club with your hands and arms. If you tilt your spine way left—toward the target—the club will descend more sharply on the ball. If you lean to the right, the club will approach the ball on an angle that's flatter to the ground. Second, if you pick the club up sharply with your wrists, or by raising your arms, the path will be much more vertical. If you allow your arms to swing the club around you more, the path will be much flatter, like a pilot leveling out a plane in preparation for landing. If you're having a lot of trouble with your shots around the green, I bet your body is tilted to the right, and you're lifting the club steeply with your hands in the takeaway. I believe it's easiest to play short game shots when the club is working on a shallow plane while the body stays steep, or tilted to the left.

When you start out with the shaft leaning forward and the ball back, you pretty much have to chop down on the ball to hit the shot successfully. There are situations where using your arms to create a steeper path to the ball is the right play—like when you have to blast the ball from some kind of divot. But for the most part, I think teaching that kind of technique for every chip isn't making chipping easier, but more difficult. It underestimates the average player's skill level. It also leaves very little room for error. If you don't hit the ball first from there, you're going to skull it or stick the club in the ground. The method I teach, with the club coming in more shallow, gives you more room to make a mistake without it turning into a horrible shot. A thin shot isn't going to skull across the green, and a fat shot will still have the club sliding across the turf instead of digging in. The bottom of the swing I teach travels much closer along the ground, so you've got more room for error. It cuts out the shots that move a foot or two,

(ABOVE LEFT) A neutral shaft position, straight up and down, creates the longest hitting area at the bottom of the downswing. In other words, there is a much longer piece of swing in which you can hit the ball and still come up with an acceptable shot.

(ABOVE MIDDLE) Starting with the club leaning forward, toward the target, reduces the club's loft. It helps on low-running shots, but it also requires you to make a very precise strike on the ball.

(ABOVE RIGHT) When the shaft leans backward, you increase the effective loft of the club and expose more of the bounce. I'll set up this way to hit a super-high shot.

or go screaming across the green. In other words, your average shot gets much, much better.

When it comes to the actual lofted pitch swing, I want you to focus on a few very specific feels to develop the touch for this shot. Your arms are going to travel back as little as possible, so the clubhead is moving freely in unison with your pivot. Remember that the clubhead needs to travel a lot farther than the grip end of the club. A very common pitching mistake is to pull the grip back away from the ball at the start of the swing. That moves the energy in the swing to the wrong end—the grip end—and really makes it hard to produce consistent contact.

One of the key elements to swinging efficiently is good sequencing. Think of your swing as three circles of different sizes. The first circle is your body. The next is the one your hands and the grip make, and the final one is the one the clubhead makes. Let's not make this too complicated, but the circle the clubhead makes is very large compared to the other ones. If you use your wrists properly in your short game shots, you have the best chance of developing the right sequence. If your body turns too early, or you pull on the grip end of the club without using your wrists to move the clubhead, you're going to destroy the biggest circle. The clubhead will be out of sequence. I'm sure many of you know what this mistake feels like.

If you hold the club in front of you and imagine that you're using the heel of the club to tap in a nail—with just your wrists hinging up and down to produce the tapping—now you have the feel of what the wrist cock in a pitch shot should feel like. To carry this feel one step further, stand tall and make a normal grip, then lay the shaft on your right shoulder. Make sure both elbows are folded and your hands are close to your chest. While still upright, turn to the right, like you would in a backswing. As you begin to turn through left, let the club fall to the ground, then allow it to bounce back up and sit on your left shoulder as you turn into the finish. Now you know how a good wrist hinge feels in a pitch shot—or in any other shot, for that matter.

Be sure to keep your hands close to your body and let the weight of the clubhead generate the energy. Don't force it with your hands. Combine that hinging with a body turn and the club moving back on an arc and you've got the basic pitch move down. Once you put this feel in action, you'll be letting the weight of the clubhead produce most of the speed on your simple pitches around the green.

The shot becomes relatively simple once you capture the feel of your pivot and the clubhead release working together. The key to knowing that your lower-body pivot is working properly is finding a balanced finish position on each shot. Your left knee will be relatively straight, and your right knee will be turned in and almost touching the left, with the right heel off the ground. If

Your goal is to keep the bounce on the bottom of the club exposed to the ground throughout the shot. To do this, think of your "release" as the unhinging of your wrists without the forearms rolling over. See how the bottom of the club stays pointed at the ground in the left photo? If I roll the toe of the club over, I lose that skid.

you don't pivot properly, your right knee will simply move toward the target line and your right heel will stay on the ground. This is a sure sign that your weight has stayed to the right.

As the clubhead moves down toward the low point of the swing, the wrist cock you created on the way back gets released through the shot. In other words, you're hitting the nail with the heel of the club, as I described before. The left elbow and wrist then slide around the body to the left to the finish, near your left pocket. That's a big, big key. You don't want to extend your arms down the target line, and you don't want to turn your hands over as if you were hitting a topspin forehand in tennis.

If you to start swinging the clubhead end of the club with some speed, you will have solved a lot of problems before they

(ABOVE LEFT) On a good pitch follow-through, my arms travel around my body as I turn, and my hands stay low, close to my left hip.

(ABOVE RIGHT) If I don't pivot and turn, my arms have to do all the work to generate speed. See how my hands have scooped at the ball? It's way harder to hit the ball solidly that way.

even start. As long as your setup fundamentals are good—weight and tilt forward, shoulders level due to a left spine tilt—unloading the clubhead puts the bounce into the turf nicely and shoots the ball up into the air. After impact, the clubhead swings around, low and left, with your hands finishing only as high as your waist. If you jerk the grip end through, your hands will finish much too high.

Controlling distance in a pitch shot comes not from swinging your arms faster, even though that might be what your instincts tell you to do. I hit my pitch shots longer by making a longer backswing and turning my lower body faster on the downswing. My pivot is small and smooth on short shots, and larger with a more aggressive turn through on longer shots. The result is that my arms

Your hands should stay close to your body throughout a pitch swing. I like to feel as if my arms are sliding against my sides. On the downswing, my right arm moves along my right side and my left elbow bends. Swing the club in front of you with just your right arm. You'll have to use some body turn to generate speed—which is exactly what you need in a pitch shot. At the end of the swing, place your left hand on the club. It should feel like your left arm is resting near your left pocket, and your left elbow is bent and around your side.

stay at home, close to my body, and the speed required for the shot comes from my pivot speed and the release of the clubhead.

If you get the idea that you need to make a faster swing, with your arms doing most of the work, the first thing that's going to happen is that the pulling action of your left arm will send your left shoulder up, tilt your spine back, away from the target, move the bottom of your swing way behind the ball, and there it is—a fat shot, or a skull from hitting it on the upswing. Think of it as a bigger pivot and you'll start to feel the chain reaction I've been talking about. My arms almost never get up past my waist on a pitch shot

(ABOVE LEFT) By letting the pivot of the lower body pull the club around through impact, the clubhead moves in the correct sequence with the rest of the body.

(ABOVE RIGHT) Pulling on the grip end of the club in the downswing causes your shoulders to tilt back and the bottom of the swing to move too far behind the ball. You'll either hit fat behind it, or compensate too much and hit a skull.

as long as 40 yards. You really don't need as much arm swing as you think you do, as long as you're using your lower-body pivot, releasing the clubhead, and using your hands and wrists efficiently.

THE BASIC BUNKER SHOT

Of all the situations you may find yourself in around the green, being in the middle of a well-maintained bunker with some room to land the ball in front of the flag should be far down the list of "scary" short game shots.

But the truth is that many players at every handicap level hate hitting bunker shots—mostly because they don't understand how to make the club work the way it was designed to. They're turning what is an easy shot—with plenty of margin for error—into something difficult and stressful.

If you practice the shot I'm going to describe here, by the end of the weekend you'll be able to get every basic bunker shot out and onto the green. That's a promise. Better yet, once you get the feel for the technique, you're going to be much more aggressive with your expectations from the bunker. It's going to start to seem reasonable to get up and down from a straightforward, flat lie. Now, of course, you can still run into trouble in the sand—we'll cover more of that in the bunker-strategy chapter later on—but a majority of your sand shots are going to be just this simple.

What you're trying to do is to put the bounce of the sand wedge—the skid of metal that sticks out on the sole of the club—in position to skip through the three or four inches of contact area in the sand. That's it. If you do, the ball will pop out and land on the green. Let's talk a little bit about how to get it there.

The most common bunker technique you've probably heard from teachers or *Golf Digest* instruction articles is to open your stance, play the ball forward and lay the face of the wedge wide open. I'm not saying that technique doesn't work. Plenty of good players do just fine with it. It gets the job done in most cases, but I don't think it's the easiest or most consistent way to get out of a bunker.

I learned my bunker technique from tour player Tom Pernice when I was playing college golf. I was—and I still am—amazed at how much simpler it is to use. It might sound a little weird, but give it a try and I think you'll be equally convinced.

Part of the trouble with the "conventional" bunker shot is that opening your stance and opening the clubface forces you to estimate how much to push the ball and allow for the sidespin to get the ball on target. I prefer to set up square to the target line and aim the face either square or just slightly open. Spread your feet very wide—wider than they'd be if you were hitting a driver—but tilt your spine slightly toward the target, not away from it like you would with a wood. Your knees will bow slightly, almost like you're sitting in a chair. Keep your ball position more toward the middle of your stance—under your left armpit—but set up farther away from the ball, so that you have to bend over more and the club's grip end is lower to the ground than you're used to.

The forward spine tilt toward the target is the crucial part of the setup. Get it right and the shot is so easy that it's almost magic. If you set up the conventional way, with the ball way forward, the tendency is to drop your right shoulder. This encourages you to dig the club into the sand too far behind the ball, or worse yet, blade it over the green when you try to compensate for that. To feel the proper tilt, try this: Set up with your feet shoulder-width apart and bend your knees. Hold your club in your right hand. Now slide your left hand down the side of your left leg until you touch your left knee. You'll have a nice spine tilt to the left.

With my spine tilted slightly left (and my weight on my left

Traditionally, players have been taught to play a bunker shot from an open stance and use an extremely open clubface. I think that just adds complexity you don't need. I set up square to the target and open the face just slightly. The bounce on the bottom of the club will do the work.

side), I actually set up with my hands back, behind the ball. In other words, the angle of the shaft is pointed back, away from the target, about an inch. It's not dramatic, but it's definitely back and not at 90 degrees. This increases the effective loft of the club dramatically, and fully exposes the bounce. You're able to set up square to the target line and aim exactly where you want to hit it, without opening your stance and the clubface and having to make that rough calculation for a lot of sidespin.

When I actually swing the club, I'm making a very narrow swing—which means my elbows stay soft, and my hands remain close to my body—instead of a wide swing with a straightened left arm. I'm essentially picking the clubhead up with my wrists and hands, while keeping my hands close to my waist. This allows me

The critical part of hitting a bunker shot is making sure you have your spine tilted slightly left at address, toward the target (1). This prevents you from dropping your right shoulder through impact and making the club dig into the sand. Notice how my hands are slightly behind the ball—this creates more loft. My backswing is narrow—I'm turning my chest, but my weight is staying on my left foot (2). Then I slap the ground behind the ball by unhinging my wrists (3).

....

to move the clubhead end fast, like I'm cracking a whip or snapping a towel. I like to feel a "cup" in my left wrist—the top of the wrist joint bent like a "V" as you look down on it—on both the backswing and follow-through. If you bow that wrist (by pushing the joint out in the other direction, like an "A"), you're exposing more of the leading edge of the wedge, which will cause it to dig instead of slide through the sand.

During the backswing, your right elbow slides back along your right side as you turn your hips. You're going to keep your weight left, so that's definitely going to feel like a reverse pivot—like you're tipping too much toward the target too early. That's natural, and it's the feel you want. On the downswing, you simply throw the clubhead by releasing the angle in your wrists and then slap the sand with the bounce on the club. You want the clubhead to pass your hands before you hit the ball. You want to sense the grip stopping before impact, so you're putting "high" on the ball as opposed to "drive," which comes from moving the grip with more speed, like you do on a full shot. Like any other shot, you want to resist trying to scoop the ball in the air with

By keeping a "V" shape in the top of my left wrist all the way through the finish, I'm exposing the bounce on the bottom of the club throughout the shot. That makes the wedge skip through the sand instead of dig.

....

your hands. Hitting down on it with speed is what makes the shot go up in the air.

By maintaining my spine tilt the same way throughout the swing, I can hit the sand much more precisely—right where my head is positioned. When you lean back at address or make a big weight shift back and then through, the spot you hit in the sand can vary by as much as five or six inches. That's just not consistent. One time, you'll hit it really fat and short, and the next time you'll hit really close to the ball and hit it too far. Once you get stable on your left side, you can really control where you hit the sand, and you'll be able to do some different things with your shots by making slight changes in your ball position. The closer I hit to the ball and the more I accelerate the clubhead, the higher the shot will go and the more it will spin.

The first few times you try this shot, you might blade a few because you aren't used to all the speed you're now generating with the clubhead. Once you realize how little effort it takes to produce enough speed to shoot the ball out, you'll relax and start concentrating on slapping the sand. Then you'll be getting up and down more than you ever thought possible.

THE LAG PUTT

We all want to make more putts. That's obvious, right? But even if you didn't make more putts, you'd take being able to consistently leave your twenty-, thirty- and forty-footers within two or three feet of the hole, wouldn't you?

Good lag putting is the underrated secret to taking a tremendous amount of stress out of your golf game. And it's a way of cutting handfuls of shots off your score without making any dramatic changes in your mechanics.

I wish I could give you some kind of chart that says exactly how hard to hit each putt. That exact kind of chart doesn't exist, but I *can* give you a relatively simple method for leaving more of your lag putts in tap-in range.

The first key to good lag putting is to make consistent contact, in the middle of the putter face. I know that if I can help you understand good technique and get you to consistently hit it solid, your brain is going to help you lag it the right distance. I want you to get out of the way of your talent.

How do you do that? By understanding how your hands should work in the putting stroke. Let's talk about your putting grip.

I teach the reverse overlap putting grip I learned when I was a kid. I believe this grip will allow you to have great feel and the ability to swing the putter freely and on-plane without any manipulation. Although I do want your hands to go on the putter in a neutral position, like we discussed with the pitching grip, there are some critical differences in the way the grip sits in your hands and fingers.

In the pitching grip, I described how the grip sits down in the fingers, so you can have the freedom to use your wrists to create speed. Your putter grip needs to keep the forearms, wrists, and hands all in a straight line—matching the angle of the shaft coming up from the putterhead—to get the putter to move on the right plane during the stroke.

Your grip also needs to be different on the putter than it is on other shots to enhance the feel in your fingers—the most sensitive part of your body. Your hands should be on the putter in a natural position relative to how your arms hang in front of your body. When that happens, the putter will swing in front of you on a natural path, without any manipulation necessary.

Like the pitching grip we talked about, a good putting grip has your hands parallel to each other, and in a neutral position. The back of your left hand and the palm of your right hand are square to the target. But most people hold the putter in a way that gets their hands working against each other, instead of flowing together. In right-handed players, the left hand is usually shifted into a too-weak position (turned toward the target), while the right hand gets too strong (turned away from the target). If that left hand is weak, the face of the putter tends to open on the way though impact, which causes pushes and pulls. The easiest way to make sure your hands are in a neutral position is to let your arms hang down naturally and see what position your hands fall into. That's basically the way they should match on the putter—so there's no manipulation.

In addition to having the hands neutral, you need to position

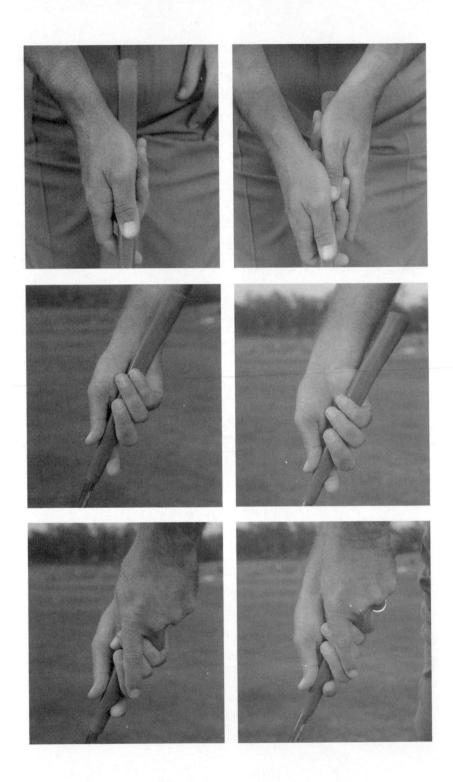

(ABOVE LEFT) I put my right hand on the putter first. My thumb runs down the top of the shaft, and there's some space between my fingers and the grip itself. Nothing feels clenched or restricted. My right palm is facing the target, and the contact points are the lifeline and the fingertips. Notice that my right index finger is slightly separated to create a soft pinching motion between my finger and thumb, like I'm holding a pencil.

(ABOVE RIGHT) I overlap my left hand so that the nail on my middle finger rests against the start of the lifeline in my right hand, and the index finger on my left hand runs down the outside of the fingers on my right hand.

(MIDDLE) In a good right-hand grip, notice how the handle runs along my lifeline and in line with my forearm. This grip will allow you the freedom to swing the putterhead with some freedom in your wrists, without manipulating the putterface (left). When I hold the putter like a 9-iron (right), the handle angles out below my forearm. This promotes the closing of the putterface if you get your wrists involved.

(BELOW) With both hands on the club, you can see the difference between a putting grip—in the lifelines (left)—and a standard iron-shot grip down in the fingers (right). See how the tops of my wrists are arched on the right? That angle has to be retained during the stroke if I want to be consistent. The good grip on the left has fewer variables.

the handle of the putter in the right place in your palms. In full shots and pitch shots, you need your wrists to hinge to add power to the swing. In putting, you may not use your wrists to add a lot of power, but the joints have to be relaxed enough to allow the putterhead to swing. While the pitching grip I showed you (and the grip you'd use for your full swing) has the handle of the club in your fingers, a good putting grip has the handle angled across your palms. From the target line, you'd see the putter come up from the ground and stay in line with your forearms. On a pitch shot, with the club in your fingers, an imaginary line from the grip end would extend below your forearms and point to the middle of your stomach. With the putter along your lifelines, and in line with your forearms, it's easy to swing the putter along the right plane and path.

I use a reverse overlap grip on my putts—my left index finger extends outside my right hand, on top of the knuckles of my right hand. In comparison, the little finger on the right hand sits between the knuckles of the index and middle fingers in the regular overlapping grip you'd use for a full shot. The main key is that your hands and arms should feel soft and responsive, not tight and restricted. Hold on to the putter with a soft grip—but with enough pressure so that you don't drop it. You want your wrists, elbows, and shoulder joints to be tension-free.

I'll tell you right up front that if you're used to holding the putter tightly, this light grip pressure is going to be a big change. It might feel like you've got less control over the putterhead, and that the club is flopping around through impact.

Actually, the opposite is true. By controlling the club with your fingers—the most sensitive part of your body—you're actually giving *more* control and feel to the shot. In other words, you're letting it happen to *make* it happen. You'll just need some time to calibrate the new feel. And the feel will come, too—I promise. If you can sign your name, you can develop touch and distance control in your putting.

This kind of grip gets the top of your forearms aligned along your target line. It's a lot like pointing a gun. If your left forearm gets higher than your right at address, you're going to lose the putt right if you don't make some other compensating move, like closing the face of the putter at address or flipping the face closed with your hands through impact. The opposite is true, too. Get that right forearm higher than the left and you'll have a tendency to pull putts left. You'll have to use your hands to compensate for that move, too, by holding the face open through impact. As you might have guessed, that isn't the most consistent way to putt. When those forearms get misaligned, it's really hard to take the putter back on the right path and get the ball to go where you want it to. If I can get you to follow only one piece of advice when it comes to your grip, it'd be to set your hands so that the forearms are aligned. That can offset a lot of other errors.

When it comes to your stance and setup, I'll continue with my "neutral" theme. If you and I were having a conversation on the practice green, you wouldn't stand there with your feet spread far apart, or so close together that they were almost touching. The same should be true for your putting stance. Your feet should be shoulder width apart or even a little bit closer together, so that you're in a comfortable, balanced position. A relatively narrow stance also helps the shoulders turn slightly with the stroke, not rock up and down as they would from a wide stance.

I also like you to be tilted forward toward the ball from the hips, not slumped forward with a curved spine or standing too upright. Tilting from the hips will let you swing the putter very easily on a good path and release it with no extra effort. Your arms will extend and swing under your body, and not get trapped up against it. From a slumped position, your elbows actually get too far behind your body, and you're forced to manipulate your hands to hit a putt. A too-upright setup isn't as common, but when it happens, you're forced to rock the shoulders up and down instead of turning them. It's also an awkward, nonathletic position that doesn't let you take advantage of your natural reflexes and senses.

From a nice, tilted position, your eyes should be aligned so that they're just inside the ball. Contrary to what you've probably heard, research shows that the vast majority of good putters have their eye line inside the ball, not over it. Scotty Cameron shared with me that for right-handers, the left eye needs to be one inch inside and one inch to the right of the ball. The way you check that is to get into your posture and hold a ball next to your left eye. Let it go and it should land inside the target line an inch and just to the right of the ball on the ground. I believe this simple fundamental matches the fact that golf is played while standing to the side of the ball, swinging on a tilted plane.

A good grip is going to put you in good position when it comes to your arms and shoulders, but it's important to keep these other setup fundamentals in mind as well. Your arms should feel very relaxed and sit close to your sides at address. I

The tops of my forearms are like the alignment sight on a gun. If you put a shaft on top of them, it should run parallel to the line you want the ball to start on. My shoulders, hips, knees, and feet are all parallel to the target line, and my eyes are just inside the ball.

have a very conscious feeling of my elbows being "soft" and rest-ing near my rib cage at address. You also want your shoulders to be relatively level with the ground, not tilted so that one is much higher than the other. A common mistake is to get the right shoulder too low in the setup, which promotes a shoulder rock instead of a turn during the stroke. Again, you're trying to set up very neutral at address, so that you won't have to make any compensations, and so that your weight is evenly spread across your feet from left to right and heel to toe. You should feel like you can stand in your putting stance as long as necessary with-out losing your balance or shifting from foot to foot.

One thing you will notice about moving to a neutral setup is that it will be much easier to maintain consistently. If your old putting setup had some unconventional pieces to it, like a big shoulder tilt at address or an exaggerated strong grip, you would have had to make subtle adjustments to your stroke every time you played just to get all the moving parts working in the right sequence.

The next thing we need to talk about is the shaft angle of your putter at address. By pressing the shaft forward (toward the tar-get) or pulling it back (away from the target) at address, you're changing the shaft angle. Many bad putters struggle because they lean the shaft backward, away from the target, at address, which pretty much guarantees that they'll start their stroke from the wrong end of the putter, the grip. It also pretty much guar-antees you will make inconsistent contact. At minimum, I like to have the shaft angle at 90 degrees (straight up and down, when looking from a face-on angle) at address, but I really want you to start with the putter pressed forward, toward the target. This encourages you to swing the putterhead away first on the back-swing, which is what we're looking for. If you do press the putter forward, just make sure you don't let the clubface open when you do it. Keep the face square to your target line.

I like the putter to lean slightly forward, toward the target, at address (left). Just make sure you don't open the face when you shift your hands forward (right).

After paying all this attention to your grip and setup, don't get careless with your ball position. I like the putterface to be in the middle of the stance, with the ball obviously just ahead of it. If the ball position gets too far forward, you'll run the risk of shifting the shaft angle backward to get the putter behind the ball at address. Move it too far back and the putterhead doesn't have time to fully release, and you'll start pushing putts to the right. Again, a neutral position—with the hands and putter in the middle of the stance and the ball slightly forward of center—will make it easier for you to make a stroke without any compensating moves.

Of course, you can have the greatest grip and setup in the world, but if you don't have good alignment, you won't be able to translate the setup—and your read—into a stroke that sends the ball in the direction you want it to go. I highly prefer square alignment—so that the forearms, feet, knees, hips, and shoulders are all parallel to the line you're trying to putt on. The quickest way to check those alignments is to hold a club across each one. If those lines get crossed—say your feet are open to the target line, but your hips and shoulders are square—you're going to create inconsistencies in your stroke. That adds a lot more guessing to putting than I think is necessary.

At least once before every tournament I play, I find a place on the practice green that gives me a ten-footer with no break. I make sure my alignment is good, and I hit straight putts to that practice hole. It's a way of recalibrating my eye, to make sure that when I've got putts with break out on the course, my feet, knees, hips, and shoulders are all on the same line. You need to check yourself at least as regularly, because alignment—and ball position—can get out of whack very easily. It's one of the most common things I adjust with the tour players I see—and it's something that happens to them without them really noticing. It's frustrating, because your stroke can feel really great, but the putts just won't drop—and it's all because you aren't aimed correctly. Tour players ask their teachers or caddies all the time to watch for ball position and alignment. Ask your local teacher or golf-savvy buddy to give you a look every once in a while and check for consistency.

Now you're set up correctly. But how do you get the ball to go where you want it to go? There are two pieces to that—distance control and green reading. Let's start with distance control.

All the mechanical adjustments I've been talking about in this section are designed to get you to hit the ball consistently in the putter's sweet spot, with the club moving on a good swing path. Making consistent, solid contact has a magical effect on your ability to judge distance. That might sound flip, but it isn't: Your

These pictures show how much the putterhead moves for a long putt—this one is a forty-footer—in relation to the handle. Many players make a common mistake: They make the same size swing for a long putt, but try to move the putter faster. That's a common cause of inconsistency. Instead, make a bigger backswing and follow-through for a longer putt. The power you generate will be smooth and consistent. You can also see the putterhead swinging on an arc—in frame 1, the face is open in relation to the target line. In 2, it is moving toward square, while in 3 and 4 it is closing. It's important to remember that this isn't happening because of any conscious twisting of the hands. It's occurs naturally when the putter swings on the shaft plane, which causes a slight arc.

brain makes a very powerful connection to how far the ball goes when you make consistent contact. It learns to predict distance very well. With an inconsistent stroke and off-center contact, your brain doesn't know how much power to deliver to the swing.

You want to preserve this instinctive connection between your brain and its ability to judge spatial relationships and the putting stroke itself. A lot of players break the connection with their pre-putt routine and rob themselves of some fantastic built-in skill. They read a putt and get a feel for the distance, then walk up and address the ball and stare down at it for twenty or thirty seconds.

The first piece of the distance-control puzzle is to make solid contact. Line up the logo on your ball with your target line and make your stroke. The logo should roll straight along the target line. If it wobbles, you're hitting the ball with a glancing blow.

Meanwhile, the visual connection between their target and the physical motion of the putting stroke is deteriorating. By the time they putt, they've essentially "forgotten" how hard to hit it.

To take advantage of your instincts, reduce the time between the end of your pre-putt routine and the actual pulling of the trigger on your stroke as much as possible. You want to see the line, judge the speed, and then make your stroke while the "image" of the stroke you need is still burned into your mind. In my routine, I consistently start my stroke five seconds after I finish my read

The action of tossing a ball underhanded, from your fingertips, has the same feel characteristics as a long putt. You can improve your sensitivity to the connection between distance and effort just by walking around a green and tossing balls to the hole.

and begin getting into my stance. The best example of a putter on tour with this style is Aaron Baddeley. Once he's into his routine, he doesn't waste any time.

Another way to reconnect yourself to the athleticism you're automatically built with is to simply walk around a practice green with a ball and toss it underhand to different holes. A putting stroke isn't too different from this underhanded toss. It's just that a lot of players make it too complicated.

Along those same lines, I'll usually have a player I'm just starting to work with begin by hitting long putts across the green with just the right hand. Why? Because the only way to get the ball moving is to sling the putter in an underhanded throw move—a move that is much closer to "natural" athleticism than anything in a contrived, jerky stroke.

The second piece of the puzzle is reading the right path the ball should roll on to the hole. Of course, that path depends a lot on how hard you hit a putt, but the basics of green reading come down to being observant and connecting what you see with what you do in your set-up and stroke.

We'll talk a lot more about green reading in Chapter 7, but let me take distance control a step further by sharing some of the technical data I've found on tempo and timing. Understanding it will give you so much better distance control—which is even more important than green-reading skill.

I have been fortunate to always have a smooth stroke, even though some people would say it has a little pop or hit to it at impact. Way back in junior golf, when I was working with Ken Lanning, my first teacher, we talked about having good tempo. But it was Fred Griffin at Grand Cypress who helped me understand how to measure tempo and timing. In my mind, tempo and timing mean "smooth." Fred was my instructor in 1993, when I had my best year on the Nationwide Tour (known then as the Nike Tour). Fred and Dr. Ralph Mann had done a study with

When you only have one hand controlling the putter, you automatically start swinging it in a more natural, athletic way. I use this drill to help clear students' heads of mechanical thoughts.

....

several of the best putters on tour. They found that there was a very strong consistency to the time that elapsed from the start of the stroke to impact on any length putt.

Through the years, many golfers, like musicians, have used a metronome to keep the beat or tempo of a stroke. The idea is that when you find your perfect tempo, you start back on a beat and then make contact with the ball on the next beat.

Over the past three years, I've learned a lot more about this concept while working with the developers of the SAM PuttLab. PuttLab uses ultrasound to measure what your putter does during a stroke. I'll talk more about this in Chapter 9.

The PuttLab measures in milliseconds the backswing time, the start of through-swing to impact time, and also the entire forward-swing time. Now that I can show my students this data, they can break free of making the same size backswing on every putt.

My stroke has certainly sped up over the past few years, probably because my life is so much more hectic. I spend so much more time traveling and talking faster than I did years ago. That being said, I still remain very consistent no matter the length of putt—900 milliseconds from when I start my stroke back until impact. This means that on a four-footer, my backswing is small and moves slowly. On a fifteen-footer, the backswing size increases, but so does the speed, and this remains the case as I move on to longer putts.

Don't miss this one important point: The speed and size of my backswing is always changing in relation to how far I have to hit the putt.

When people struggle with long putts, the backswing on a forty-footer has the same pace—and the same length—as the one they use for a twelve-footer. They don't produce enough length or momentum for the shot, so they have to "hit" at the ball to give it enough juice to get to the hole, and that messes them up. They make poor contact and leave it short, or they blast it ten feet by the hole.

Chapter 4

THE THREE HARDEST SHORT GAME SHOTS, MADE SIMPLE

· ·

The three shots we talked about in the last chapter are going to help you negotiate a large majority of the situations around and on the green. Basically, they're shots that are the building blocks for routine pars.

In this chapter, we're going to talk about shots that have the potential to turn into double or triple bogey. These shots—an intermediate pitch shot, a chip shot from the rough close to the hole, and a long bunker shot—are the ones that turn into second short game shots because you blade it over the green or leave it in the bunker. The extra short game shots you have to hit after a bad result are the shots that really do damage to your score.

My goal here is to give you the best, most efficient strategies and techniques to hit these three shots successfully—and my definition of "successfully" depends on the shot and your overall skill level. At the minimum, I'd like to leave you with the ability to hit these three shots out of trouble and onto the green. As you get better, you're going to be in a position to go on offense with some of these shots—where your expectation is to hit it within three or four feet of the hole.

If you're a 15-handicap player, I'll bet that you can look at the scorecard after every round you play and peg a triple bogey that came from a big mistake on a difficult short game shot. If you minimize the damage by simply advancing the ball onto the green and two-putting, you can turn that triple bogey into a bogey. Shaving two shots here and there with some simple adjustments to strategy and technique is the way a 15-handicapper turns into a 9 in a month or two.

Before we get into a discussion about these three specific shots, let me address one question I get a lot when it comes to learning "difficult" shots. When I start to talk about more challenging shots, players will often ask me if I expect them to be able to hit shots that tour players hit. Well, yes and no. Do I expect you to be able to execute a shot at the same level as a tour player, and do it consistently nine times out of ten? Of course not. Tour players have tremendous talent, and they can do things that most people can't. That's why they play for big money.

But the tour players who make the hard short game shots look so easy do so because they've already worked out the most efficient way to hit the shot, and then they let talent take over. And I strongly believe that no matter what skill you're talking about—from hitting a delicate pitch to learning how to drive a race car—the easiest way to get better is to learn the most efficient way to get the job done. If you owned a business, and I had a month to come work with you and learn how to run your company, would you show me how you do it, or would you give me a completely different game plan from the one you used, and throw away all the experience you earned and the mistakes you learned to avoid? I think you'd want to show me your best tactics, right away.

So yes, there's a difference between what an "expert" can do and what a "beginner" can do, but *anybody* can improve by learning the most efficient techniques.

That's a super important point to make.

I believe the average player has more than enough talent and feel to learn the same techniques that tour players use. You might not get up and down from 40 yards eight times out of ten, like Sergio Garcia does, but I promise you that if you use his technique, you can go from one time out of ten to four or five out of ten. That's a big, big deal.

THE 30- TO 50-YARD PITCH

How you feel about hitting an intermediate pitch—a shot that's less than a full swing, but more than a short greenside shot—says a lot about your overall short game mechanics. The player who makes a big arm swing with no body rotation is always going to struggle with this shot, while a player who makes a smaller arm swing and controls the distance by the speed of the pivot loves hitting it. That's just as true for a tour player—and there are plenty of them that don't like this shot—as it is for a 20-handicapper.

At the amateur level, players make two huge mistakes—mistakes that make this shot way, way harder than it has to be.

First, when the average amateur player walks up to his ball 40 yards short of the green, with plenty of green to land the shot, he mistakenly sees it as a shot he has to hit high, and fly the ball almost all the way to the flag.

But if I was playing this shot, I would picture my ball flying onto the green a little less than halfway to the hole and then running on the ground like a putt. The shot I hit definitely has backspin on it, but I'm not trying to do anything to make the ball hit and check and stop. My goal is to hit the ball as low as I can for the shot at hand (so I can get the ball rolling like a putt), and hit it solid. Hitting it solid will produce some backspin and make the ball check a bit when it hits for the first time, but it will still roll out.

Second, very few amateur players understand how to control

distance by using the lower-body pivot. The most common mistake is to open the stance and make a big, full arm swing—as if you were hitting a full shot—but without any body turn. Then, the only way to hit the shot the right distance is to slow the club down on the way through impact. In reality, a 40-yard pitch takes about a 25-percent-size arm swing, with a nice, gentle lower-body turn through impact.

What do I mean by pivot? A pivot is a small hip turn back and through, which you can feel mostly in the way your knees work. As the club is moving back, the right knee moves away from the target line while the left moves toward it, and vice versa on the downswing. The mistake players make is that the right knee goes forward, but the right heel stays on the ground. That causes you to fall back as you swing. Instead, let the right ankle roll in, the right heel release, and the right knee move up and toward the left.

If you picture a long metal bar superimposed over your spine and anchored in the ground, you pivot *around* the fixed bar, like you would if you were tossing something underhanded.

In fact, you can take a golf ball and toss it underhanded down the range first with a frozen lower body, then with a gentle pivot. You'll immediately feel the difference. When your lower body is stiff and unresponsive, it's hard to generate enough energy to move the ball very far. It's also awkward and unathletic, and you're robbing yourself of a lot of feel and sensitivity.

When I'm teaching juniors here at Grayhawk, we'll walk around to collect the balls at the end of a drill, and I'll ask them to hit little one-handed chips to move the balls into the middle, where they're easier to pick up. Without even telling them *how* to hit those little shots, they load the club nicely in the backswing with a wrist hinge and make a little pivot to generate the speed on the clubhead. Then I'll go and work with an adult who has had twenty years of lessons, and he's strangling the grip and

(ABOVE LEFT) When I pivot correctly, my right knee "bumps" and follows my hip turn. It moves toward my left knee, like I'm throwing a ball underhanded.

(ABOVE RIGHT) If I just bend my knee but don't turn, my knees stay in the same position relative to each other, and I've held my weight back. This will cause inconsistent contact.

shoving it back and forth with stiff arms and no pivot. A lot of my teaching is designed to help people get out of the way of the athleticism they already have. I want to give you permission to do what would come natural if you didn't know so much about golf. Why can you turn the putter around and hit the ball with the back edge? Because you're taking golf out of it. You're taking what you think you know, and what you're trying to do, out of the motion.

Once you understand that the size of the lower-body pivot is the "accelerator" on an intermediate pitch—the faster you pivot, the farther the ball travels—then you simply need to hinge the club back and let it release as the pivot happens. A simple way to feel what your hands need to do—or not do—in this shot is to practice setting your wrists and letting them release.

(TOP) My setup for a mid-range pitch shot is the same as it would be for a full shot with a short iron (1), but with a slightly narrower stance. I'm not choking up on the grip. The size of the shot you hit isn't controlled by how fast you swing your arms, but by how much you pivot and how fast you turn back through the shot (2). Notice how much my hips have turned through the shot (3). A common mistake here is to keep the lower body quiet and swing the arms fast.

(MIDDLE RIGHT) Here, I've made a huge arm swing—as if I were hitting a full shot. This leads to a big tug on the grip on the downswing and a glancing strike on the ball That leads to all kinds of compensating mistakes.

(BELOW) On a pitch shot, your arms should follow through the same amount as your turn. In the first picture, the handle of the club has stayed pretty much in front of my belt buckle as I've turned through a 40-yard pitch. If my arms dominate the swing, like in the second photo, my hips stop moving and my arms sling way up over my shoulder.

....

With your hands in front of you, use your left hand to push the handle of the club toward the ground. That will lift the clubhead into the air, and set your wrists in a great hinge. Now, just let the club fall back to the ground. Don't push it down or help it in any way. Just let the weight of the club do the work. Add some shoulder turn and a lower-body pivot, let your right elbow slide back along your side on the backswing, turn through impact, and you've got it. It's really that simple.

Most players have never actually felt the weight of the club-head, or relaxed their grip enough to let centrifugal force move the clubhead end. Because we're not talking about a 300-yard shot, it's tempting to try to jerk the grip around and overcontrol the shot, picking the whole club up in the air on the backswing. If you've got some coordination, it's possible to hit some decent shots from there, but it takes a lot of compensation and effort. You can be decent, but you'll never be great. I want to share the technique that works with no compensations—the one that the greatest short game players in the world have always used.

The last element in controlling distance on an intermediate pitch shot is changing trajectory. As I said before, I prefer to hit these shots as low as I can get away with. It's always easier to land the ball on the spot I pick when the trajectory is lower then when it is higher.

How do you control trajectory? By using your wrists and forearms. When I want to hit a lower shot, I start my backswing and immediately set my left wrist with a little bow in it—so that the face is pointing more toward the ground—and I swing the clubhead more in and around my body. This move reduces the effective loft on the club and produces a flatter swing plane— and a flatter plane gives me a longer area where I can hit the ball and still be successful. I keep my arms very relaxed, with low tension, and when I make my pivot on the downswing, my lower-body turn pulls my arms around my body. This move causes the clubhead to lag behind, creating more of a bend in my right wrist. That bend reduces the effective loft of the club even more. Then, as I turn through impact, that lag gets released automatically— without any hitting or throwing move with the right hand on my part.

If you can blend the pivot with a simple release like this, you'll develop a tremendous amount of control over this shot, and a straightforward intermediate pitch with a lot of green in front of you won't cause you any difficulties. The bigger challenge comes when you're playing on a course with very firm and fast greens, and you need to hit a shot where there's not a lot of green to work with around the flag. That's a difficult, risky shot, because you have to play a high shot that lands softly and doesn't roll out as much. We'll talk more about what to do in that situation—my modified version of a flop shot is probably the best play—when we go into short game strategy in the next chapter.

The back of my left hand is a basic representation of the clubface at impact. Here, the logo on my glove is in a neutral position—straight up and down. If I want to hit a shot with more loft, the back of my hand (and the logo) need to point up into the air more at impact—which happens when you start out with the clubhead forward of the hands at address. For a low shot, I'd do the opposite, and turn the back of my left hand more down, toward the ground.

IN ROUGH, CLOSE TO THE HOLE

The mix of conditions for this shot makes for an interesting dilemma. Say you're 10 yards from the hole and only two steps off the green, but in deep grass. The ball doesn't have to travel very far, but you have to swing hard enough to avoid getting your club tangled in the grass. And it's not like the shot gets much easier when the grass is shorter. Even from a good lie, the close-to-the-hole chip shot is one tour players probably struggle with more than any other shot because they have a lot of different options and it's hard to pick the best one.

Let's break this shot down into two flavors—one from deeper grass, and one from a good lie in short rough or fairway grass.

The deep grass shot usually comes about because you "short-sided" yourself on an approach shot. Say the pin is ten steps away on the green, on the left side, and you go for it but pull your approach shot just slightly. The ball hits the green but dribbles off through the fringe and settles in deeper grass just a foot away from the fringe.

Now you have to hit a shot that flies only about six or ten feet, but you have to get enough speed on the clubhead to get it through the grass.

To get a feel for how to play this shot, you have to understand how to swing the clubhead versus move the handle. If you make a big motion with the handle of the club and swing the entire club way back, you've got enough momentum to hit a shot 30 yards. You can predict the result: Because your brain knows that the shot only needs to go right over there, you slow the club way down on the downswing and scoop with the hands to try to pop the ball out of the grass. Either you stub the club in the grass and move the ball about a foot or you blade it across the green.

The best way to play this shot is to think of it as a little bunker shot, where you use the bounce of the club to skim through the grass and splash the ball up and out of the grass. This also has the added benefit of reducing how precisely you need to hit the ground. Like a bunker shot, you can hit anywhere from three inches to an inch behind the ball and get a good result.

To get a feel for this motion on a shot from grass, set up like you would for a bunker shot, with your feet shoulder-width apart and your weight favoring your left side. Your hands and the club should be in the middle of your stance. Start the swing by setting your wrists first—moving the clubhead end away from the ball—and making a small body turn. On the downswing, feel as if you're slapping the bounce on the bottom of the club across the grass with your right wrist—that sidearm throwing move we talked about in the section on intermediate pitches.

Because it's a short shot, it's temping to focus just on your arms. After all, how much power do you need? But if you just swing your arms and don't make a pivot with your lower body, the club will lift off plane and you'll have to redirect it on the downswing. That's obviously a recipe for inconsistent contact.

Focus on that little lower-body pivot and keep your arms and wrists super relaxed through the swing. You want to feel as if your body turn will be enough to sling the clubhead through impact without you having to add any more force to it with your arms. Once you start pulling and shifting the handle, you take all of that soft, natural clubhead movement away. You're also stealing all of your feel. The tension takes away all of your natural responsiveness and touch.

When I watched players like Seve Ballesteros hit these shots, I was always impressed with how soft everything looked—soft arms, soft legs. Nothing was rigid. Tilt your shoulders toward the target a little bit to help keep your weight forward, and avoid adding a lot of tension to your arms by reaching for the ball. Set up so that your posture allows you to keep some bend in your elbows, and then work your elbows along your sides in both the backswing and downswing. I like to feel my right elbow slide toward my right hip on the backswing, and then my left elbow work around past my left hip on the forward swing. Neither one of Steve's arms ever straightened during one of these delicate shots, and I don't think you can go wrong copying a genius.

(LEFT) The setup for a lob shot is the same as your bunker address position: Your feet should be shoulder-width apart, with your weight mostly on your left side and your hands slightly behind the ball. You can actually use the exact same technique as you would for a basic sand explosion shot.

(MIDDLE) My arms and wrists remain soft through the lob shot—neither arm ever straightens or tightens. Notice how much my wrists are hinging. The end of the grip stays pretty much in front of me.

(RIGHT) My wrists are unhinging aggressively to produce the speed that shoots the ball up in the air. My left wrist is completely cupped, and my left elbow is bending and moving along my left side. See how the face of the club is pointing straight up in the air?

Now, just because I don't want you to make a big swing with the grip and your arms doesn't mean you don't need to generate speed with this shot. Remember, it's going to work the same way a bunker shot does, with the club sliding through the grass and making indirect contact with the ball. When you get the feel for hinging and unhinging your wrists to generate that speed, you'll feel an interesting combination of things—that you aren't working as hard as you did before, and that the clubhead is moving faster than you expected. That's just where you want to be, because the added speed on the clubhead is what will help it get through the grass and generate height on the shot.

Believe it or not, if you're a step or two from the fringe, you can even use a putter on this shot, even from the deep grass. Move the ball back slightly, so you're hitting down on it before you get to the lowest point of your swing. You want your hands to be forward, and you want to hit down on the ball so it jumps up and forward just enough to crawl out of the tall rough. The momentum will run it down to the hole. You're going to use more wrist than a normal putt, and produce almost no follow-through. Resist the temptation to try to hit up on the shot to launch the ball. Even a putter has enough loft to take care of this on its own. By hitting down on the ball, you'll make it take a big hop after impact—then land and roll out like a putt.

From a better lie, the problem is much more one of visualization than technique. At the tour level, good players walk up to a shot and almost immediately see the best option. From that point on, everything they do is focused on executing the shot they see. It gets more complicated when the player has a variety of different choices.

For example, let's say you hit an approach shot to a green where the flag is up, and there's a wide, flat, closely mown chipping area in front. If you leave your shot just short of the green, you've got a variety of shots you can play. You could hit a basic

From a step or two off the fringe, you can play a shot with your putter fairly easily—even from deeper grass. Make a normal putting stroke, but don't try to scoop the ball out of the grass. The loft on the putter is enough to pop it out on its own. If anything, you want to hit down a little bit on the ball.

chip shot, but there's not much green to land the ball on. You could putt, but there's enough fringe between you and the hole that the ball might not track exactly true. Or, you could play a more lofted shot back to the hole—but we've already talked about how those shots are less predictable than others.

The average player might not have quite as many shots to choose from as a tour player, but indecision is still a killer. I'd rather have you pick a slightly more difficult shot and commit to it than approach an easier shot with indecision and only half-heartedly hit it, just hoping to get it up there "somewhere."

Indecision is easy to spot when I'm watching a player hit a shot. From a good lie that is close to the hole, most players should be hitting what I call an "offensive" shot—one that they feel good about hitting close or even making. When you're not sure about what shot to hit, you play a "defensive" shot—one where you just hope for the best. When you get defensive, you have a tendency to try to baby the shot with an arms-only swing. The swing plane gets too steep, which leaves just a tiny area of the arc where you can catch the ball solidly. If your timing isn't exactly right, then you're going to hit it fat or thin.

So what shot should you pick? I hate to cop out, but it really does depend on the situation. If you're under pressure—say, to get up and down to win a bet with a buddy, or to qualify for the club championship—and you're looking at a firm, tight lie, you might feel a lot better about putting the ball up there than using a club with loft. Of course, my goal is to get you feeling comfortable enough with your short game to have a choice. I like to chip under those circumstances, because you can carry the ball over some of the uneven ground that could kick it off line.

Some players hit a sort of combined version of a chip and a putt with a hybrid club. The loft on the hybrid gets the ball up and over some of the uneven fringe grass, but the ball lands quickly and rolls out like a putt. The flat sole on the hybrid also skids along the ground, so you don't dig in and lay sod over the ball. If you do pick the hybrid option, use the same setup, grip, and stroke as you would with your putter.

The conditions between you and the flag determine a lot about what shot you play—especially when you're close to the hole. Here I'm hitting three dramatically different shots. First, I'm hitting a fringe putt (1) that obviously rolls the entire distance. This shot works great on fast greens, and when you're nervous. When the fringe conditions are good, you can also hit a chip shot (2) that rolls more than it flies. This takes some of the fringe out of play. You can play a pitch (3) if it's important to get the ball to the putting surface before it rolls out.

....

LONG BUNKER SHOT

In the last chapter, we talked about how to hit a basic "blast" bunker shot—where you hit the sand behind the ball and not the ball itself. And trust me—even if you don't love playing from the sand right now, a shot from a good lie in the flat part of the bunker will be pretty easy for you.

Of course, there's a limit to how far you can hit a blast shot from sand. Using my 58-degree wedge, I can hit a blast shot about 30 yards and still keep it under control. Your comfortable blast distance might be a little bit longer or shorter, but the question is, what do you do when you have a shot longer than blast distance, but shorter than, say, 80 yards, where you could make a full swing?

You *could* try to hit a standard blast shot but with a different club, like a 9-iron. If you pick that shot—and it's not my favorite, because you have to be pretty precise with it—you have to make sure to make a big turn and generate enough clubhead speed to prevent the club from sticking in the sand, since a 9-iron doesn't have the same kind of forgiving bounce as a sand wedge.

I'll hit the shot with my sand wedge, but instead of playing a blast, I'll get into my chip setup (which we talked about in the last chapter) and essentially hit a "skull-chip"—where I'm trying to hit the equator of the ball with the leading edge of the wedge. Just like the other shots we've been talking about here, I'll control the distance not with the size of my arm swing, but by the speed of my pivot.

I set up with the ball a little bit back of center. When I'm trying to intentionally skull the ball, the goal is to hit the ball on the downswing with a lofted wedge, so it comes out low and with a lot of forward momentum. As you can imagine, it's a shot that will roll out a lot, so it won't work if you have a lot of trouble to carry in front of you.

(ABOVE LEFT) A long bunker shot—40 yards or more, when a standard explosion shot won't get there—is different than a standard explosion bunker shot in that you're actually trying to hit the ball first, before the sand. I set my ball position just back of center to encourage that chip shot–like contact. To check your ball position, hang a club from the buttons of your shirt.

(ABOVE RIGHT) That's the center of your stance. Play the ball just back of that.

(BELOW LEFT) I play the clubface relatively square on long sand shots, with the shaft leaning forward to hit the ball first—just like I would on a chip shot.

(BELOW RIGHT) For a long bunker shot, I'm basically making the same swing I'd use on a chip shot. My hands stay low and move around my left hip through impact. The clubhead never gets higher than my thigh.

If you practice this little skull-chip shot with your sand wedge, you might find that you have more control over it than your standard blast shot. You might even want to use it from closer to the flag when you have some green in front of you to let the ball run out.

One thing to keep in mind is that you don't have to swing nearly as hard as you'd expect. You're delofting the wedge at impact, and the ball is going to roll a lot. Relax and take a small, compact backswing. Making clean contact on the ball first is more important than smashing it with a lot of power.

Another attractive thing about the skull-chip is that it's a lot less dependent on the specific club you choose. Hitting it with a 58-degree wedge will give you a little more height, but you could switch out and hit it with a 9-iron for a longer shot with a lot more run. If you play at a course with fast, dry conditions—and you don't have any trouble in front of you—there's no reason you couldn't play this shot from 50 or 60 yards away from the green and let it roll up there like a super-long chip. Hey, all that matters is the result and whether or not you can hit the shot consistently, not what the shot looks like.

Chapter 5
SHORT GAME STRATEGY

· ·

We've spent some time going over the basic shots you need for most short game situations, and the ones that will bail you out of trouble. But understanding *how* to hit a variety of shots is only part of the battle.

The essence of short game strategy is seeing the variety of shots you could hit in a given situation, and then picking the one that fits a combination of two important factors. First, you have to have some confidence that you can execute the shot. Second, the shot you pick has to fit reasonably well with what you need to accomplish.

Even after you've worked your way through the shots in this book and gotten good at them, you're still going to have a favorite—one you feel that you can hit consistently well. My favorite short game shot is a low runner with my 58-degree wedge that I chase onto the green and let roll out like a putt. When I have a good lie in fairway grass—or any other situation where I can make clean contact on the back of the ball—I'll pick that shot over any other one.

If my lie isn't as good, or if I need to fly the ball a greater percentage of the total distance of the shot, I'll hit the basic pitch shot we talked about in Chapter 3. By swinging with some more speed and getting the bounce on the bottom of the club

When picking a short game shot, you're weighing a variety of factors—the change in elevation between you and the hole, where you want the ball to land, how much danger there is to carry between you and your landing spot, and the green conditions around that landing spot.

involved, I can not only produce more height, but I can power the club through a sketchy lie.

From a bad lie, where you aren't sure if you can get the club on the ball, your approach is going to be a lot more like you'd hit a bunker shot. I'm going to talk more about that in the trouble shots section in the next chapter.

These are three pretty cut-and-dried shots that cover a majority of the scenarios I'm going to face—the low runner, the basic pitch, and the basic bunker shot. You don't need to learn a dozen different shots and keep a cheat sheet in your bag to figure out when to hit them. If you learn a few shots, and develop some feel with them with a few different clubs, you'll be way ahead of the game.

We're going to talk about some of the most common short game situations in this chapter, but what happens if the best shot

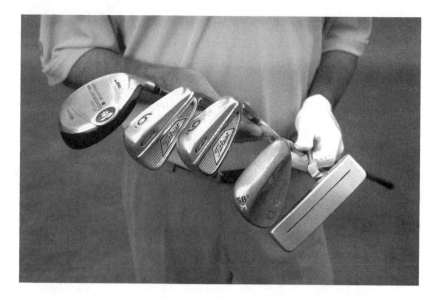

You don't need dozens of different short game shots to be a good player. If you learn a few basic shots, and can hit them with a variety of clubs, you're going to have a tremendous number of options. Then, the trick is learning when to use them...

for the situation isn't one you like to hit? I'd always prefer that you pick a shot you're comfortable hitting, even if the situation isn't perfect for it. For example, if you have a shot from a good lie in the fairway, just short of the green, but you have two different tiers to deal with on the green, a tour player would probably choose to fly a shot far enough onto the green to take the tiers out of play.

But if you're a fantastic chipper, and you really enjoy hitting shots that run along the ground, I'd tell you to hit that shot every time, even if you ran the risk of leaving it a little farther from the hole. Your average result is going to be better with the shot you like to hit than the one you're not as comfortable hitting. And you have a chance of dumping the lofted shot at your feet or blading it over the green—assuming you really aren't comfortable—when you bring the pitch shot into play.

The same advice holds true for pressure situations. When you get nervous, the best thing you have going for you is a go-to shot you're comfortable hitting. That might mean leaving the ball ten feet from the hole instead of potentially hitting it to two feet, but sometimes playing a little away from the hole, where you have some room to hit a basic chip, is easier on the nerves.

You might think that this kind of advice only applies to you if you're an accomplished short game player with an overall handicap lower than 10. I couldn't disagree with that more. By having a very clear understanding of your strengths and weaknesses and picking shots that have a higher probability of success, you're doing the one thing that will lower your handicap the most.

I watch dozens of 15- and 20-handicap players play every year in pro-ams. I see no more than a handful of those players assess their situation and pick the right shot, only to mess it up because of bad technique. It's far more common to see the average player walk up to his short game shot with no real plan or idea about where he wants the ball to land, and then hit a shot that is a kind of mix of techniques—and mess it up. If all you did was think about where you wanted the ball to land, make your plan, and hit the shot you liked to hit, you'd slice six or seven shots off your handicap. And that's without improving any of your technique.

Obviously, if you get comfortable with a few more shots, you're going to be able to play more offensively instead of defensively. If you're a good chipper and a good pitcher, you'll be able to attack more hole locations and play less conservatively. But my advice about first choosing your shot holds true regardless of your overall short game handicap number from Chapter 2.

Achieving the right balance between your comfort level hitting a certain shot and how well the shot fits the situation is important, but another critical piece of the short game puzzle comes *before* you even hit a short game shot.

Think about the last approach shot you hit from the middle

of the fairway from, say, 150 yards. Did you see the flag on the green and aim right for it? Probably. Most players get within that range of the green and basically ignore the conditions that surround and encompass the green—unless there's something dramatic going on around up there, like a huge water hazard.

But every green has places on it and around it that are better to land on than others, and it's important to be aware of them. If you can't hit it tight to the hole—and let's face it, most shots aren't going to be within ten feet—you need to know where the next best and worst places to be are.

I'll give you an example from a tournament round I played recently at the Pebble Beach Invitational. I get to the 10th hole, a 430-yard par 4, and I hit my tee shot in the fairway, 170 yards from the hole. The 10th hole runs right along the ocean, so you can't miss that green right, otherwise it's a lost ball over the cliff. In front of the green on the left, there's firm fairway that tends to kick the ball toward the green. If you land the ball pin high, the ball will bounce hard on the firm green and go over, where you've got a tricky pitch. I've played that hole probably fifty times, and my miss strategy is burned into my head—short and left is the good mistake.

So I took a club that will go a maximum of 165 yards, and probably more like 160 in the cool conditions, and aimed just left of the flag. I knew that if I hit the shot perfectly, I'd be on the green just short of the hole. If I missed it just a bit, it was going to be left and short, and I'd still have a chance for the ball to kick up on the green.

The ball flew a little short, hit just in front of the green, and trickled on the front. I made a routine two-putt from there, and took my par.

That's the way it should work, but I didn't keep it up on the 11th, a 373-yard par 4. That hole has a very narrow green that slopes from back right to front left. I hit my tee shot in the fairway, and

I had 160 yards to the flag. My ego was telling me that I could fly it right back to the hole and make it stop. But in reality, as firm as the greens were, if you landed a shot near the hole, it was going to go over the green and leave you with a pitch to a downhill hole location—basically a one-out-of-ten up-and-down. I landed the ball within a foot of where I wanted—but a foot too far—and the ball trickled into the back fringe. I hit a great chip under the circumstances, to seven feet, but I missed the putt and made a bogey.

It doesn't matter what your handicap is, or how much control you really have over your ball from the fairway. You're going to be better off if you understand where the good and bad places to miss are—whether you successfully pull off the shot you planned one time out of ten or eight times out of ten. Relatively speaking, you're going to save shots by being in an easier place to take fewer shots to get into the hole.

If you're hitting to a green that has a giant, deep bunker pin high to the right, and you're a terrible bunker player, you need to be doing whatever you can to make your miss short and left. If you're a 20-handicapper, that might mean playing a club that can't get all the way to the green. You have a better chance to get up and down—or, at worst, take a chip and two putts to get in the hole—from a flat lie in the fairway than from the bottom of a deep bunker. If you're a scratch player, it might mean playing away from a flag for the fat part of the green and being content with two-putting.

I caddied for Jay Haas at Bay Hill, Arnold Palmer's PGA Tour event in Orlando, the last time Arnold competed in the tournament. Jay was paired with Peter Jacobsen and Mr. Palmer for the first two rounds, and the experience of being around for those two days was one of the coolest I've ever had in golf.

The course was playing really long, and Mr. Palmer was swinging with everything he had and hitting it about 230 off the tee. The most fascinating thing to watch was that he hit his ball really, really straight all day, but from the tournament tees, he was left with long approaches on almost every hole. Although he couldn't reach the green, he took dead aim at the pin every time—not once changing his strategy based on where his ball was going to land. He played 36 holes without once aiming where there was a runway or a safe place to miss.

Why did he do that? Because he's Arnold Palmer, and people didn't come to see him lay up. They weren't as interested in seeing Arnold Palmer put together a strategy that would have allowed him to shoot 75 or 76—which he certainly could have done. They wanted to see him try to hit the hero shot, and they didn't care if he shot 84.

Arnold Palmer can still see in his mind the great shots he's played in his prime, and for sure, he should play whatever shot he wants in his event. He has earned that privilege, and he knows his place in the game.

But if you're swinging away at your approach shot without at least some sensitivity about where the best place to miss might be, you're just being foolish. You're expecting a perfect outcome that really might only happen one time out of fifty. You can choose to play golf that way if you like, but you're going to have to expect a lot less in terms of score.

When you walk up to your approach shot in the fairway, you should be analyzing the green for what I call "hard positions." Start with the big ones: penalty strokes. If you make a mistake, are you going to be in a lake, or in an unplayable lie? Those are also the easiest to identify.

The other hard positions relate mostly to two factors—places where you can't get a club on the ball cleanly, and places where you don't have much room on the green to land your shot.

Is there one side of the green that has deeper grass, or a deep bunker with a high lip? Does one area around the hole have long, wispy grass that could snarl the clubhead as you swing? Is one particular area around the green a low point where water always drains? The grass is usually lusher there, and you could get a lie with grass on top and mud below—another tough one.

Generally speaking, you'd rather be hitting a short game shot uphill to the hole instead of downhill. Which way does the green tilt? You'd obviously want to favor the side where the ball stays below the hole—especially when the greens are running very fast. If you're hitting a downhill chip or pitch, you might not be able to stop the ball because of the slope or the green speed, and you might not be able to swing with enough speed to put spin on the ball to get it to check up. Then you're pretty much resigned to playing it safe and past the hole, versus risking leaving yourself a tricky downhill putt.

At the end of this process, you should essentially have a rough map of the green complex in your head with color-coded areas blocked out. The green areas are places where it's okay to miss. Yellow areas are the iffy ones that come into play when you need to be aggressive, and the red ones are simply dead.

It's completely possible to have a situation where there isn't a safe way to even try for the green. The 14th hole at the TPC Southwind in Memphis is a downhill, 220-yard par 3. It's got water two thirds of the way around its tiny green. Now, I don't have a high 3-iron shot, so I've never even aimed for the green. I always aim left and try to run it up onto the chipping area short of the green where I have an easy chip. My goal was always to take double-bogey out of the picture.

You might be reading this and thinking to yourself, if it was that easy to decide where to miss, I'd just hit it right at the hole. That's true to an extent, but don't make the mistake of thinking this advice doesn't matter if you aren't shooting in the 70s. As I said before, everything is relative. Even a tour player doesn't have control over every single shot. But you can peg your expectations to your talent level, and to the length of shot you have into the green. If you're a 20-handicapper and you're holding a long club in your hand, like a hybrid or a fairway wood, you should be looking for a big area to miss in. In fact, as unromantic as it might sound, you're probably better off hitting a shot in the fairway short of the green, where you can hit an easy pitch or chip for your next shot. If you're that same 20-handicapper and you have a 9-iron, it's more reasonable to expect that you could favor one side of the green or another.

Now that we've covered the things you should consider before you actually get up around the green, how do you decide which of the shots we've been talking about—a low runner, a pitch shot, or a bunker-style lob shot—to actually use?

The number one consideration is lie. If you have a clean lie on short fairway or fringe grass, you have your first green light to pick from a variety of shots. If the lie is sketchy—maybe the ball is sitting down in a depression, or on the edge of a divot—the determining factor is whether or not you can hit the back of the ball cleanly and fully. If you can, you still have the full menu of shots to choose from. If there's something between you and the ball—rough, the edges of a divot, some dirt—then you need to hit more of a trouble shot. We're going to talk about those in the next chapter.

Let's start from the premise that you have a perfect lie. The next determining factor is the path you have between you and the hole. If you're on the same level as the hole, height-wise, and there are no obstacles between here and there, the safest and most effective play is to hit a shot that lands on the green pretty early and rolls out like a putt.

When I get to my ball, the first thing I do is take a walk along the route to the hole, to start to visualize where I'd like my shot to land. I'm checking out how firm or soft the green is. Is the grass shiny in one direction or the other? If it's shiny as I look at the hole, it means I'm hitting with the grain, and the ball will roll out more. If it's shiny when I'm looking back at the ball from the hole, it means I'm hitting against it, and the ball will want to check up when it lands.

If I'm playing a shot that will roll out, I pick a place to land the ball that's about the size of a basketball hoop. I want that spot to be in a place where the green is pretty flat, so I can hopefully get a true bounce. Then I read the rest of the green from that landing spot the way I would a putt. Many players make one of two (or both) critical mistakes when they aim a chip shot: They aim at the flag and forget about the lay of the land on the green, or they pick a good landing spot but don't pay close attention to how the ball is going to roll out from that spot. And as your ball slows down—hopefully near the hole—it's going to take more of the break that's there, just as it would on a putt.

Once I have my landing spot picked out, I'll literally step off the distance between that spot and my ball and count off in yards. One full step is roughly a yard, so I have a pretty good measure for the distance the ball needs to fly in the air. One of the most productive practice sessions you can have is to step off five yards, ten yards and twenty yards and place a headcover or other marker at each one. Then go back and practice hitting short game shots that fly each distance. As you play more and more using these techniques, you'll find that your sense of what kind of speed you need for a given distance to a landing spot is going to click in more and more precisely.

When you start to encounter obstacles between your ball and the hole, you're going to have to consider a shot that flies more of the total distance than it rolls. When I talk about obstacles, I mean a lobe of deep grass or bunker, or a tier on the green. Tiers are the most common obstacle—the hole is on a different level than you are, and you have to negotiate a slope to get there. A lot of times, it's better to fly the ball up on top of the tier, to the same level as the flag, because this takes the guesswork out of rolling it up the hill.

I'm sure you've seen tour players like Phil Mickelson and Ernie Els hit pitch shots up onto a tier that hit and zip to a stop with backspin. Although you may see these guys on tour, or even a few of the best players at your club, spin the ball this way, most of us need a different option. You don't have to do anything special to make it happen. On the basic pitch shots we've been talking about over the last few chapters, you're relying more on the height of the shot to stop the ball, not backspin. And keep in mind that if you aren't using a multi-cover tour ball, you're not going to get that kind of spin. (Not to mention the fact that grooves on wedges are going to be a lot less sharp in the years ahead, thanks to the USGA. But that's another story....)

Regardless of whether or not the green you're playing has tiers, it's always a good idea to read what is going on behind the hole in addition to what's happening between your ball and the hole. Sometimes you have a tier or greenside slope rising behind the hole and providing you with a nice backstop. If I'm playing to a middle pin with a big tier going up behind it, I know I can hit a shot a little more aggressively, because if it rolls past the hole, it will come off the tier and feed back.

Grain and green hardness are also going to influence your decision, just like they did on the bump-and-run shot. When you're playing to a back tier from significantly below the hole and you're going into the grain or landing the ball on a soft green, the safest option is to fly it up there. The conditions are going to help it stop.

Under faster conditions, you could consider playing a shot that takes a little more practice. I like to hit a pitch-and-run shot that hits into the face of the tier. The tier takes some speed off the ball, and it trickles up onto the correct level. It's definitely like a bank shot in pool, in that you need to practice to get a feel for how much power you need.

No matter what shot you pick to try to get close to the hole, you have to understand another concept—leave—which is also a lot like playing pool. "Leave" is the shot you have after you've played the first one. In pool, you're doing more than just sinking balls in the various pockets. You're trying to sink balls and put the cue ball in good position to take the next shot.

Your short game works exactly the same way.

The goal is to execute a good chip or pitch and leave yourself in position to have a relatively easy putt. If you've always struggled with your short game, you might think that "anywhere up there" is a fine leave. I hope we can get you to the point where you aim a little higher than that.

One of the key concepts of leave is understanding when to sacrifice trying to hit the ball close to the hole and instead concentrate on avoiding a score-busting mistake. Essentially, you should always be prepared to calculate when it's time pick a shot where the worst result is a two-putt.

If I get out of position like I did on the 11th hole at Pebble Beach, and I know I have a difficult, slippery downhill shot in front of me, my automatic first thought is that whatever I do, I'm not going to leave the ball short. Why? Because a slippery downhill, sidehill eight-footer is no bargain, either. I'd rather have a ten-footer straight uphill than a six-footer down the hill with four inches of break. The six-footer is easy to hit four feet by, which leaves you in position to miss that one, too.

Again, this advice isn't just for 10-handicappers, scratch players, or tour guys. I think most players underestimate their ability to play for the next shot. I just came away from playing a pro-am, and I saw the guys on my team playing too passively or too aggressively. I'm sitting in the cart and looking at the scorecard, so I know where they get their handicap shots.

If the 20-handicapper on my team hits the green in two and he knows he's getting a shot on the hole, you can see it. He's all fired up, and that mindset puts him in a place where he blasts his first putt six feet by. He didn't have any kind of plan, or what-if strategy for the fact that his putt was on a slick downhill slope. All that was going through my mind was that if he lagged up there and tapped in for par, we'd get a shot. The same kind of thing happened a few holes later when he had a shot from the fringe. I watched him try to hit a high pitch—a shot he wasn't great at—when a putt from there would have had a much, much better chance of success. He's just introducing more risk and higher scores into the equation. Small things like that can add up to a dozen strokes per round.

The basics I'm sharing here work for tour players, and they work for 20-handicappers. But average players are going to get way more out of improving their strategy choices, because they're the ones who don't really *have* a strategy right now. If I can just get you to see some of the choices, you're going to benefit, even if you can't quite execute the strategy every time just yet. If you start picking better shots every time, you're going to get way more payoff on the ones you *do* execute. Sure, there'll be some double-bogeys in there. We all make them from time to time. But you'll stop throwing away so many boneheaded shots.

Chapter 6

BUNKER/TROUBLE SHOT STRATEGY

. . . .

Even if you've done your best planning, like we talked about in the last chapter, you're going to end up in a less-than-ideal situation every once in a while. That's part of golf. It's how you handle things from there that determines your score.

And there's more of a reason to group bunker shots and trouble shots together than just the fact that they're the only things "left" in the short game conversation. Once you've learned how to hit the basic bunker shot we talked about in Chapter 3, you'll not only know how to hit a bunker shot, but you've also learned a shot that will work for almost any sketchy lie.

Like we talked about in the last chapter, you determine what kind of shot you can hit—and how aggressive you can be with your expectations—by the kind of lie you have, and whether or not you can hit the ball cleanly. If you can't make clean contact on the ball, either from the sand or from a bad lie around the green, you need to explode the ball out of trouble by hitting behind and using the bounce. And that's the perfect description of a bunker shot.

Does this mean you can do the exact same thing for every bunker and sand shot and not really worry about any subtleties? Yes and no. You could just use a basic bunker technique and get good results—which would be a tremendous improvement if you are, say, a 15-handicap short game player. But by taking that basic bunker technique and adding some diagnosis about your lie in the sand or grass, and making some slight modifications based on what you see, you can become an exceptional sand and trouble-shot player.

Let's start diagnosing sand conditions, and what they mean for the shot you want to hit.

Three main factors determine what kind of lie you will end up with in the sand—moisture, sand depth, and the trajectory of the shot that ended up in the sand. In terms of moisture, sand can run the gamut from fluffy, like powdered sugar, to sludgy, like wet cement. The more moisture the sand contains, the firmer it will be, and the more likely the ball is to stay up on top of the sand. In drier, fluffier sand, the ball tends to nestle down.

Because sand depth is related to moisture, you should base your shot decision on the layer of sand just below the surface—not what is sitting on top. After all, a standard bunker swing sends the bounce on the club skipping through the sand. Understanding how deep the sand is—and whether or not the layer below the surface is soft or hard—helps you pick your shot. It's very common, especially early in the day, to have a bunker shot where the thin top layer of sand is wet from dew, but the sand underneath is fluffy. If you get too casual and decide that you're hitting from firm sand, you'll make a mistake, and probably leave the shot short for reasons we'll discuss in a minute.

How do you make the diagnosis? After all, the rules say you can't test the condition of the sand by touching it with your hands, or by taking a practice swing that disturbs the sand surface.

Start with the mark your ball made when it entered the sand. The trajectory of the shot has a lot to do with it—especially in soft sand. The steeper the trajectory of the shot you hit into the bunker, the more likely the ball is to stay in its own crater when it lands. In other words, if you hit a fairway wood or long-iron shot into the bunker—or any shot that was rolling before it went in—you're more likely to have a lie where the ball is sitting on top of the sand. If you hit a short iron shot and the ball lands in the sand, it's coming down almost vertically, and could stay in its own crater.

When you survey your shot, you can see by the crater just how deep, soft, or moist the sand is—before you even decide which shot to hit. The most important clue comes when you actually step into the bunker to hit the shot. Your feet will give you a tremendous amount of information about the sand conditions. If you sink in and make deep footprints, you're obviously dealing with soft, fluffy sand. If you can walk on top of the sand, like a wet beach, you're dealing with firm sand.

Why does it matter? You can use the same kind of swing for each shot, but to get the best results, you should change where you make contact with the sand based on its firmness. The firmer the sand is, the closer you can hit to the ball—an inch or less behind it—and the less speed you need to use to get the ball out. The club will skip near the top of the sand, and you'll have firmer sand between the club and ball, which will push it faster. Now, firm is one thing and concrete is another. You might run into a bunker that's basically just petrified dirt. You can play a basic bunker shot from that lie, but you have to be careful not to bounce the club off the hard surface and blade it. From a super-firm lie, you could play a simple chip shot, or even putt the ball out.

From fluffy sand, you want to hit farther behind the ball, with more speed, because the soft sand gives way more quickly and the club will tend to penetrate deeper into the sand. That puts more of a glancing blow on the ball. If you swing with some speed, you can get away with hitting the sand as much as three inches behind the ball, as long as you're hitting the sand with the bounce of the club exposed.

(LEFT) The best bunker lies consist of firm, relatively shallow sand. You can propel the club through, but the sand provides enough resistance so that the club doesn't dig in too deeply.

(RIGHT) On a firm sand lie, the ball sits on the surface, as if you were playing from a wet beach.

The quality of the lie you have is going to determine a lot about what your shot will do when it lands on the green. The closer you hit to the ball—for a firm lie, for example—the less sand there is between the club and the ball. The less sand there is, the more friction you produce on the ball, and the more backspin you create. So a standard bunker shot from a good lie in firm sand will tend to land and check up.

From a fluffier lie, the loft of the shot is going to have to do more of the work stopping the ball. The more you set the clubhead ahead of your hands at address, the more loft you will generate on the shot.

When you start to deal with poor lies in the bunker—plugged, buried, or fried-egg lies—you're going to get shots that will fly out lower and roll more. That's just the cost of the mistake or bad luck that put you in the bad lie in the first place.

Where should you aim when you play a "standard" bunker shot from firm or fluffy sand? The answer revolves around backspin, so to speak. From a good lie, I fly all of my shots pretty close to the hole, because I put a lot of backspin on my bunker shots. You need to determine what the "standard" roll out is for you from different types of sand, and then adjust according to the quality of lie you have. Your average bunker shot might run out twenty feet. If the hole is ten feet onto the green, that might mean you just accept that you'll be ten feet past it—unless you want to take the risk of hitting a more lofted shot.

What kinds of things impact your ability to make clean contact in sand? Let's go over the two basic "trouble" lies in the bunker, and how you should adjust your basic bunker swing to account for them. The first is a "fried egg" lie, where the ball is sitting in a big, splashed-out crater. There's no sand directly around the ball, but it comes into play an inch or so behind and in front. For a normal shot, I keep my clubface pretty square. In this case, I'll open the face dramatically—45 degrees—to expose even more of the bounce. Then, I'll hit the sand behind the back edge of the crater, hard, and move a lot of sand. The open face helps the club power through the sand without digging, and the added loft shoots the ball up in the air.

In a plugged or buried lie, the ball is jammed into the sand, almost as if someone had stepped on the ball and pushed it in. The traditional way to hit this shot has been to close the face, play the ball back in the stance and chop down on it to gouge the ball out. For me, that's always been too much of a hit and hope kind of technique. You don't really have any control over how the ball will run out.

Instead of using the closed-face technique, I teach players to hit this shot with the clubface wide open (75 to 80 degrees) at setup. Use a medium to narrow stance, with the ball just inside your left heel. Use your wrists to pick the clubhead up very

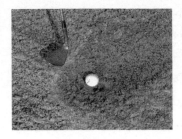

(LEFT) In a fried-egg lie, the ball is the yolk, while the crater it has created is the white. The ball sits down slightly in its hole, but there are uneven spaces in the sand around it to contend with.

(MIDDLE) The conventional way to deal with a buried lie is to play the ball back in the stance and gouge the ball out with a closed clubface. You don't have much control on this shot.

(RIGHT) I like to open the face and hit behind the crater and explode the ball out with speed. This shot gives you more loft and a softer landing.

steeply in the backswing, then release the club back sharply into the sand about an inch and a half behind the ball. At this point, you must stop the clubhead just past impact. You may want to even try to recoil the club back out of the sand, like you're cracking a whip. This downward pressure on the sand will squeeze the ball out more softly and with more control than the closed-face technique.

Now is a good time to talk about the different stances you can encounter on a bunker shot, because the advice I have about how and when to hit them applies to the technique you'll use for most other trouble shots, too.

You can be the most aggressive when you have a clean lie and the ball is sitting on a slight upslope, because the uphill lie is going to help shoot the ball high into the air. In that situation, I'm going to hit pretty close to the ball—about an inch away— and aim to land the ball in a bucket within five feet of the hole.

As the lie gets more uphill, the ball is going to shoot higher and higher when you hit it. That means you have to swing harder to make the ball go both longer and higher.

If the lie is dramatically uphill—knee-height or higher—balance becomes a big factor. If you get too active with your body, you'll have a hard time making contact in a consistent place in the sand. It's important to set your weight mostly forward and leave it there throughout the shot.

When I'm playing a shot from a super-steep uphill lie in the sand, I'll try to pinch pretty close to the ball and continue to swing down after impact—to the point that the club sticks in the slope after impact. I want the pressure from the clubhead entering the sand to shoot the ball up and out of the bunker.

Downhill lies are more difficult, for two reasons: First, you're working against the slope to get the ball airborne. Second, you'll have the tendency to hang back on your right side to keep your balance through the shot. And as I'm sure you know by now, that's exactly the opposite of what I teach from the bunker. And hanging back like that is particularly bad on a downhill lie, because you'll either hit way behind the ball or overcompensate and blade it over the green. On this shot, make sure to keep your spine tilted toward the hole, widen your stance, and move your right leg back, away from the target line. This will help you pick the club up more abruptly and finish low down the hill and still make solid contact with the sand. You do have to accept the fact that this shot isn't ever going to have much loft on it.

Assuming you don't have to do anything crazy like stand with one foot out of the bunker, sidehill lies in sand follow the same rules as their counterparts from the grass. If the ball is above your feet, you need to adjust your ball position back, just behind middle, and expect that you'll hit it left of where you aim. You can adjust your target accordingly, or you can open the face slightly—which has the added benefit of giving you a little more

(ABOVE) The slope of the sand is going to help my ball up into the air, but I still set up with the clubhead ahead of my hands and most of my weight on my front foot (1). On the backswing, my head doesn't move. I'm just making a level shoulder turn and cocking my wrists (2). I throw the club with my hands and plow the club down into the sand. No lifting or scooping (3).

(BELOW) On a downhill bunker shot, I set up so my shoulders are parallel to the ground—which means I need to bend my right knee and move my right leg behind me to accommodate my spine tilt (1). Just like the uphill bunker shot, I turn my shoulders without shifting my weight off my front foot (2). It's important to swing down through the sand and around my body (3). If you try to lift the ball, you'll lean back on the downswing and hit the ball thin.

The trajectory on a downhill bunker shot is going to be low no matter what you do. You have to plan for that when you pick out your landing spot.

loft. If the ball is below your feet, you have to make sure to tilt over more from the hips and keep that spine angle through the shot. The common mistake on that shot is to straighten up on the downswing, which will cause you to hit the shot thin. If you stay in your posture the right way, you can expect the shot to drift to the right.

A ball's proximity to the lip can also cause some shotmaking problems. If you're close to the back lip, you have to deal with the edge of the bunker getting in the way of your backswing and downswing. To play that shot, you have to set up like you would for the downhill bunker shot I just described, but make your backswing even more narrow by immediately cocking your wrists—not swinging the club back with the arms at all. The goal is to chop down behind the ball with the bounce on the bottom of the club. You're going to have to come almost straight down to clear the back lip, so it's important to have the face open so that it can slide under the ball a little bit.

Playing from near the front lip is an easier shot—and one that you can use in a lot of different situations around the green. Take a very wide stance and bend over from your hips so your hands hang much lower than usual, making sure to keep your spine tilted toward the target. Open the clubface so that the bounce is lying flat on the ground, and set up so the shaft is angled away from the hole. All of these things by themselves add loft to a shot. Assembled together, they make it so you can basically hit a ball straight up in the air if you need to. During the swing, your goal is to get your hands—not your arms—moving very fast, and to splash the bounce of the clubhead an inch behind the ball.

You can take this exact same setup out of the bunker and use it from the rough for a lob shot over an obstacle. The taller grass will behave pretty much like sand would, and the low hands, open face, and forward shaft position will help you shoot the ball up into the air. On this shot, I'm trying to swing the clubhead with my wrists early enough in the downswing so that the clubhead begins to pass my hands at impact—with the bounce of the club still pointed at the ground. If you roll your arms over when you release the club, you'll smother the ball straight into the grass. Concentrate on letting the left elbow fold around your body through impact and finishing with your left wrist cupped.

Unless you need the extra loft to clear an obstacle, most of your trouble-shot strategy around the green is going to involve diagnosing the lie and interpreting how your ball will come out of the trouble. That will give you a sense for how careful you need to be. For example, if your ball rolls up against the fringe, you have a variety of shots you could use, but none of them are super-

The setup for a lob shot is the same as my basic bunker setup, but I bend more from the hips and lower my hands. This increases the loft on the club (1). I hinge my wrists aggressively, but don't shift my weight off my front foot. See how the club is moving around my body on a flat plane (2)? My hands stay low and the back side of the club slides across the grass, shooting the ball up in the air. I'm feeling like I'm sticking the butt end of the club in my left pocket (3).

high risk. A tour player might choose to take his sand wedge and hit the equator of the ball with the leading edge of the club to produce a shot that rolls out with some topspin. A 15-handicapper might putt it, but try to hit the top half of the ball, or he could even use a hybrid—which, in this situation, is basically a putter with 20 degrees of loft. We're talking the difference between holing out and leaving the ball ten feet from the hole.

But on the other hand, there's a real difference between a pitch shot from a great lie and a pitch shot from a deep divot. Depending on how poorly your ball sits, you might have to aim away from the hole and hit to an area where you have a lot of green to make a mistake.

The kind of grass the ball is sitting in has a huge impact on what you can expect from the shot you need to hit. Take the

When the ball comes to rest against the first cut of rough, you can play a variety of shots depending on your comfort level. From shorter grass, hold your sand wedge like a putter and hit the equator of the ball (1). You'll be able to hit the ball more solidly than if you use a putter (2), because the sole of the wedge slides through the longer grass better than a putter will. But for a higher-handicap player your worst miss with the putter will be much more playable than a bad miss with the wedge. From the edge of deeper rough, you can still use the wedge (3) or putter (4), but the wedge is going to do a better job sliding through the deeper grass than the flat face of the putter.

difference between Bermuda rough and bentgrass rough. I know that my club generally goes through the softer bentgrass easier than it does the Bermuda. But if the bentgrass rough is long, you could be hitting out of grass that is standing straight up, or lying in a certain direction. If the grass is leaning toward your target, it will usually come out nicely. If the grass is leaning toward you, however, the shot will usually require more clubhead speed—making that shot one of the trickiest to hit.

How deep the ball sits in bentgrass rough also affects the shot you can hit. If it is sitting down, near the base of the grass, it's safer to use the bounce of the club and hit the ground first—like a standard bunker shot. But if the ball is up near the top of the grass, you can make a bunker-type swing and go completely under the ball. With the ball up, you have to swing the club to exactly the right height—almost like you would with your driver. For that shot, I like to hit a low, running chip. I take the wrists out of my swing and use my pivot to shoot the ball out and get it running.

The risk with Bermuda is not swinging with enough speed. The grass catches the hosel and turns the face to the left, smothering the ball. I almost always play a bunker type explosion shot from Bermuda rough, making sure to swing with enough speed to power through the grass.

Just because the grass gets shorter doesn't mean you run out of potential trouble spots. A very tight lie on a well-manicured fairway can be a challenge because there's not much grass under the ball. That kind of lie is a problem for the same reason that a lie on hardpan is tough. You feel that if you hit too far behind the ball, the club will bounce off the ground and you'll blade it.

Now, the most obvious advice is that anytime you're concerned about hitting the ground, you can play a shot where you hit the ball first—like a basic chip shot. The trouble starts when you try to lift a shot from a firm lie into the air by scooping and hanging back with your body.

The important thing to remember is that if you keep your spine tilt left, you can actually get away with hitting the ground first if you focus more on swinging the club around you instead of chopping down on it with your arms and leaning back. It's the backward tilt and the chopping move—where the leading edge of the club hits the ground first—that causes the club to crash

into the middle of the ball—not the firmness of the lie. You can actually hit a bunker-style shot off the pavement if you swing on a flat enough plane and make contact with the ground with the bounce on the heel of the club rather than the leading edge.

In fact, you can play the exact same kind of shot from a wet,

You read your divots based on how cleanly you can hit the back of the ball and how firm the ground is. When the ball is in the front of a divot (1), you have more options, because you have a clean strike. From the back of a divot (2), the club won't react as predictably when it tries to plow through the edge before it gets to the ball. A tight lie (3), bare lie (4), and dirt lie (5) are similar in that you don't have a cushion of grass below the ball. You need to either chip these and hit the ball first, or lower your hands and expose just the bounce on the heel of your wedge. From mid-rough (6), the ground is close enough below the ball that you can make a bunker-type swing without fear of going completely under the ball. If the ball is sitting on top of deeper grass (7), you need to be precise in your swing depth, like you're hitting a driver off a tee.

muddy lie as you would from hardpan and get pretty good results. Think of both shots as basic bunker shots, but move a little farther away from the ball and lower your hands. This will help you make a flatter swing, around your body, and it increases the chances that the bounce on the bottom of the club will hit the ground, not the leading edge. And just like the bunker shots we talked about earlier in this chapter, the hardness of the surface you're hitting from dictates how hard you have to swing. From a wet, muddy lie, you need to generate more speed to get through the mud and shoot the ball up. From a hardpan lie, there's nothing between the club and the ball, so you can swing easier.

The next time you go play a round for fun, hit every green-side trouble shot twice. First, hit it in the way you'd normally play it—by chopping out, or otherwise improvising a solution. Then, hit it with a simple bunker shot, adjusting how close you stand to the ball and how low your hands get to make the ball go higher when necessary. Track both results and I'll bet your average leave is better with the bunker technique. It's simpler to practice one thing, and it takes a lot off your mind when it comes to decision-making.

Chapter 7

THE PUTTING STRATEGY GUIDE

· ·

Even though you don't have the variety of shots, trajectories, lies, and club choices on the putting green that you do around it, there's still a strong strategy element to putting. And how you approach a longer-range putt from, say, twenty feet or more is just as important as it is on the other shots we've talked about. And in some ways, the stakes are even greater. With a good putting approach, you can make up for a mediocre—or even just plain bad—short game shot. And if your putting approach is bad? You're just compounding the problem.

Let's start at the beginning.

The fundamental mistake many players make is walking onto the green and marking the ball without any kind of plan. If you aren't paying attention to what is around you, you aren't going to be able to ask yourself the continuous stream of questions that all good putters ask. The answers to questions about the prevailing slope on the green, speed, grain, read, and leave—where you want the ball to finish to leave the easiest second putt if you don't make the first one—are what inform your putting "instincts."

Think about the course you play most often. You probably have a feel—and it can be a conscious or unconscious one—about what each of the greens there does. You probably know that a certain green has a big tilt from one side to another, or that another green sits lower on the property, so it's wetter and slower than the rest. You have the information, but it's not written down in a systematic, organized way.

I grew up in Missouri, playing on bentgrass greens that were pretty long. Those greens were in good shape—not shaggy or anything like that—but they were slow and pretty hilly. I developed a feel for the general speed of those greens, and my creative ability grew because I saw a lot of putts with eight or nine feet of break.

But when I got closer to college age, I started playing regional tournaments around Missouri, Kansas, and Arkansas. Some of those courses were in hillier areas, and those greens were faster and had some serious tiers on them. And in college, at the University of Missouri, we played in events in the South on courses with Bermuda grass—which was a whole different challenge for me.

I realized pretty early in my serious competitive career that I needed to figure out a better way to retain information about the greens I was playing regularly. Improving my stroke was one part of the equation, but I was never going to be able to take advantage of my good putting stroke if I didn't have a sense of how I was supposed to play shots on those greens.

So I started the basic green charting system that I use to this day. When I prepared for a tournament, I hit practice shots and played full practice rounds, but most of my intense work came on each of the greens. I'd walk each green slowly and carefully, and hit a lot of practice putts from all kinds of different spots. On either the yardage book or a series of plain note cards, I'd draw each green and make notes about where shots needed to land when the pin was in certain positions. I wanted to know how far the different tiers were from the front, back, left, and right sides of the green. I also noted whether a green tended to play firm or soft, and what kind of grain was prevalent, so I'd have more

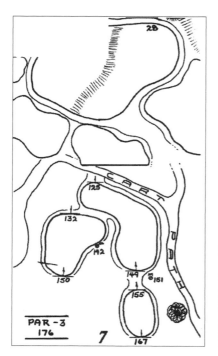

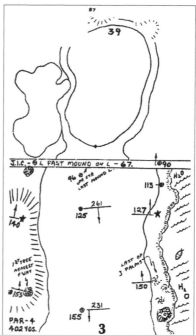

On this diagram from the yardage book for Waialae Country Club, I've marked the direction of the grain on the 7th green—from back to front—along with a reminder that the green is really fast. The note at the top reminds me that I can hit a 4-iron to the front hole location into the wind, but that the back pin is a 3-iron.

Here, grain is also back-to-front, and the note on the top reminds me that the strong grain makes chipping it from behind the hole really difficult. The goal here is to not go past the flag.

information to use when planning my approach shots and short game shots. And I also noted the prevailing landmarks around each green.

LANDMARKS

What do I mean by landmarks? If you're playing at a course where the greens have some slope, there's usually a point on the property—or in the distance—that corresponds to the "high." Here in the Phoenix/Scottsdale area, one "high" is a mountain called Pinnacle Peak. If you're playing in the northeast part of the valley and you're unsure about which way a putt breaks, greens tend to run away from Pinnacle Peak and toward Phoenix. In Palm Springs, greens tend to break toward the city of Indio, in the lowest part of the valley. In Pebble Beach, they tend to head toward the ocean.

Maybe you play your golf in the Midwest, where the greens are pretty flat and a landmark like Pinnacle Peak (or the Pacific Ocean) isn't so obvious. If that's the case, you can do a little investigative reporting. Head out to the maintenance shed and look around for the greenskeeper. He might tell you that all the greens tilt toward the pumphouse behind the 14th green, or tilt away from the expressway that runs along the east side of the course. Or you can even spend some time in the clubhouse bar talking to some old-time members. They won't have any shortage of opinions about the prevailing break on the greens. Just be sure to go out and test those opinions.

Discovering the high point in the area, like Pinnacle Peak, is a way to understand the macro, or "big picture" lay of a course, while deciphering the prevailing slope of each hole gives you a more fine-tuned view of what kind of slope and contours you're up against. On every hole, the designer usually has to follow the general terrain of the area, and he has to provide a way for the green to drain off rainfall.

If you hit a great approach shot, you might get pumped up when you see your ball sitting five feet from the hole as you walk up toward the green. Or, if you hit a bad one, you might be sulking and looking down at your feet. Both of these situations are missed opportunities. Regardless of the shot you hit, you should be looking at the green complex as you walk up. You can often see the overall tilt of the green to the left or right, or perhaps the drainage area on one side or another. If a creek or a river runs next to the green or crosses in front of it, the surface of the green itself almost always tilts toward that water—and putts will tend to break in that direction even if the designer tries to neutralize that tilt.

Now, it isn't as simple as looking at every putt and automatically playing it to break toward these landmarks and prevailing slopes. But understanding these "highs" is a way to answer the first of those questions I talked about at the beginning of this chapter. And tour players know that the guys who ask—and answer—the most questions are the ones who win.

SPEED

In a perfect world, all the greens on your course would be the same speed, and they'd be that speed every time you came out to play. Better yet, when you went to play a different course, you'd get some kind of code to plug into your putting stroke so you could automatically adjust.

Of course, it's not quite that easy.

Green speed is a function of two main factors: How tightly the grass is cut, and how firm the ground is below the grass. At

Augusta National, they cut the grass down to an eighth of an inch, then roll the surface to make it hard and firm. The result is like putting on a linoleum floor, and that's no exaggeration. At the other end of the spectrum, a local public course might cut the greens three times as high, and then water them aggressively to keep the grass healthy under the load of hundreds of rounds a day. Longer grass and moisture content—both in the ground and on top of the grass—make for slower speeds.

Green speeds even change at the same course during the same morning. If you go out and play early, in the dew, the greens will be moist and slow. By lunchtime, when the dew has burned off, you'll have to account for quicker conditions. It's also very common for the grass quality on a course to be better on some greens than it is on others. If a green is back in the trees, where it doesn't get a lot of sun or air circulation, the grass might be patchier and the surface faster. Out in the open, a green might bake in the sun, and the superintendent might give it more water to keep it alive. That water slows the speeds down. One of the most famous examples of that situation occurred at the 2004 U.S. Open at Shinnecock Hills. The grass on the 7th hole came close to dying during the tournament, and tournament officials had to splash water on it every so often to keep it alive. If you played the hole right before the splash, you couldn't keep the ball on the green. If you played it right after, you had a small chance to hold it.

It's obviously not just man-made irrigation that changes things. If it's been a wet few days, the greens are going to be damp and slow, and not just because of the extra water. The maintenance crew can't get out and cut the grass as often or as effectively when it's wet, so the grass on the green will be both damp and longer than normal, and the ground underneath will be soft. The opposite is true in the middle of the summer, when it's been dry for a few weeks—or dry for months, like it is in

Scottsdale or Palm Springs. The crew can keep the greens alive by watering them, but the desert conditions and the hot sun will still bake the greens hard.

All that information is great, but how do you translate it to the course you're playing, and the specific hole you're on? Your first piece of information comes from the practice green. Again, in a perfect world, the practice green would be an exact representation of what you'll see out on the course. Sometimes that's true, but most of the time, a practice green is slower than the real thing. Why? Because the practice green usually gets watered as frequently as the rest of the grass around the clubhouse, but it's not cut as often as the real greens. And at upscale clubs, appearance is important, especially around the clubhouse. It's important to have a lush practice green—as a kind of badge of honor. Like I said, green and lush usually translates into slow.

Still, pay close attention to your practice putting before a round to get the feel for that speed. I like to use just one ball, and hit a twenty-foot approach putt to a hole, then make the putt that's left before switching to a different target. Using one ball and holing out gives you a definite sense of speed, because you're left with the consequences when you misjudge one. It also adds some pressure to your practice, which is a great way to replicate what happens out on the course. If you drop three balls and hit a bunch of similar ten-footers, you're not connecting what happens on the practice green to what would really happen out on the golf course.

Once you get to the first green, take your time and examine the pitch mark your ball made on your approach shot. Is it a deep divot? When you fix it (and you should always fix your pitch mark, even if you don't care about green speed), take care to notice how moist and soft the soil is. On hard greens that don't show much of a pitch mark, the green speed will tend to be faster.

Like the other elements of putting strategy we've been talking about, judging speed is a matter of feeding a lot of information into your mental computer and paying attention to the results. I know that when my speed is dialed in during a good putting round, it's because I'm very sensitive to where my ball ends up during every stroke, accounting for the changing speed conditions. You can even get some of that information by paying closer attention to where your playing partners' balls end up when they putt. Are they making small strokes and knocking putts way by the hole? Are they hitting them firmly but ending up short? All of that is more information for the computer.

GRAIN

If you believe that grain—the direction that the blades of grass on a green grow—is something that only matters when you're on a course with Bermuda grass, you're wrong. Every green has grain, from Bermuda to bentgrass. You might not be able to see the grain if you're playing on super-fast bentgrass greens that are cut very short, but it's there. Your job is to figure out how much there is, and determine how much it will affect your shot.

The number-one hallmark of grain is shading. Take a lap around the green before you mark your ball. You should be able to see that the grass appears darker from one direction than it does from the other. When it appears darker, you're looking into the grain. The grass is growing toward you. If the grass appears lighter and shinier, you're looking downgrain. The grass is growing away from you.

Another way to determine the prevailing grain on a green is to look into the cup. One edge of the cup will be clean and crisp: The grass is growing away from that edge, and can be cut cleanly. The other side will be ragged—that's where the grain is headed. A slow-rolling ball will tend to be pulled along the grain, toward the ragged edge of the cup. If you're really stuck, remember that Bermuda grain moves toward the southwest. On bent greens, it heads toward the setting sun.

You're going to see the greatest difference between light and dark on heavy-grain grass like Bermuda, but the color change is there on bent greens, too. The degree of color change gives you an idea of how much the grain is going to change the path of your putt.

And just how much can grain move a ball? If I have an otherwise straight ten-footer on a heavy-grain green, and it goes across the grain, I need to aim about three inches to the left or right (depending on the direction of the grain) to account for it. If I aimed for the center of the cup, I'd miss the putt.

That's a big deal, but not as big a deal as how grain affects speed. Misreading a break by three or four inches can leave you with a tap-in. Forgetting to account for grain when it comes to distance can leave you with a difficult second putt. Yesterday afternoon, I was out at the practice green at Grayhawk, helping a high school player with his putting. I hit a putt toward a hole forty feet away, in the northeast corner of the green, which I knew was uphill and straight into the grain. My putt ended up three feet away, but my friend's putt ended up fifteen feet short. Those mistakes are the reason you three-putt, and they don't have anything to do with the quality of your stroke.

Another crucial factor to understand about grain is that your ball reacts differently when it travels into the grain than when it travels downgrain. When you're hitting into the grain and you don't hit a putt solidly, the ball will jump off line right away. You can get away with a less than solid strike on a downgrain putt, because the grass tends to carry the ball on the line on which it started.

I'm not trying to tell you that I stand there and compute the exact change in the length of my backswing to account for the exact amount of grain on every hole. I'm saying that asking questions about grain and answering them for yourself on every hole feeds into your instincts. You see if your assessment was accurate or off, and you're sharpening your green-reading "tool" for the future. You're adding information to the computer. You won't get it right away, but you're building a body of knowledge that is going to make your average putt so much better.

As you become more sensitive to grain and those putts get better, keep in mind that some putts are always going to be hard, and don't get too discouraged. If I have a forty-five-footer that is thirty feet uphill, into the grain, and then fifteen feet downhill and downgrain, I don't have much expectation that I'll lag that putt close. Those putts are hard for everybody.

READ

When you combine landmarks, speed, grain, and any other factors that affect where you want your putt to go (like wind, which can blow a putt off line if it's strong enough), it adds up to a read—or the path you think the ball needs to travel to go in the hole. Some players are naturally better at seeing that line than others, but I firmly believe that green reading is a skill you can practice and improve. Then, if you have a good stroke, you can send the ball on the line you see in that read.

I teach players to identify the high point of the break on every putt. In other words, when you pick out the way your putt is going to bend to go in the hole, the high point of that break is the top of the arc in the path. Once you've identified that high point in the break, your entire mission is to set yourself up to hit the ball on the start line that makes it go at that point. The ground takes care of the rest.

Let me take you through my process of reading a twenty-footer. I start by processing all the big-picture information—landmarks, overall green tilt, grain, speed—before I even get to my ball. Once I've made some decisions about those things, I look straight at the hole from behind my ball, then walk behind the hole and look at the putt from the opposite direction. It's much easier to see uphill and downhill movement from behind the hole than it is from behind the ball. When I walk back to my ball, I make sure to walk to the low side of the putt—the side opposite the high point of the break—and look at the putt halfway between the ball and the hole. For example, if my putt breaks from left to right, I want to look at the break from the right side of the ball (relative to looking at the hole from behind the ball), halfway between the ball and the hole. From that perspective, you get the best sense of just how much curve your putt will have.

Most players dramatically underestimate how much break to play in a putt. As a result the brain subconsciously pushes you to hit the putt harder, because the only way for an under-read putt to go in is with more speed, on a straighter line. That means, of course, that a lot of putts get blasted ten feet by the hole.

The best putters slice each read into parts. When the ball first comes off the putter, it is moving pretty fast, and it won't take as much of a break as it will toward the end of the putt, when it is moving more slowly. Your read has to take that into consideration. A slope that's right at the beginning of your putt is going to have less impact on the read than a slope that's right by the hole. On putts of twenty feet or longer, I make a general read about the first 75 percent of the roll, then go up by the hole to read the last 25 percent more carefully, because that's where most of the action is going to happen.

When you have a fast, downhill putt, you have to be a lot more careful about your read than you do with a slow, uphill putt,

(ABOVE) I start my read from behind the ball, facing the hole, so that I have full perspective with both eyes. Then I walk behind the hole, away from the ball, to see if that read confirms my original assessment. When I walk back to the ball, I go on the low side of the break—opposite the side where the ball is going to reach the apex of its curve—and stop halfway between the ball and the hole and make another read.

(BELOW) When you see break in a putt, you have to change your orientation so that you face the apex of the break (left), shown by the stake in the green. If you face the hole (right), you're going to see the putt as far straighter than it really is.

....

because the fast putt will be hit with a smaller stroke and the ball will be moving more slowly. It'll take even the slightest break. If you make an aggressive swing (making sure to hit the ball solidly), you can read less break, because the ball will be moving faster—neutralizing some of the slope.

Once you identify the break and the line you want your ball to start on, you can use your ball to help you keep to that start

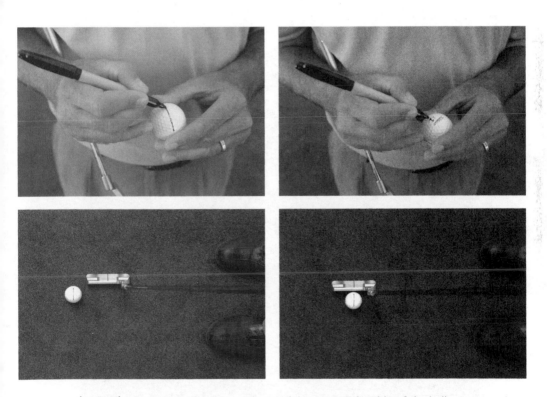

(ABOVE) I draw a marker line on the model name on the side of the ball, to create a dark aiming line. Make sure you draw the line straight. I also make another marker number the same as the one printed on the ball, so I can identify my ball from others in the rough.

(BELOW) With the marker line in place and aimed down your start line, you can go through your pre-putt routine, then set up over the ball with the line on the putter matching the line on the ball.

line. I use a marker to make a thick black line over the model name on the side of the ball (along with a big number next to the printed one on the other side, to distinguish my ball from everyone else's). When I make my read, I putt my ball back on the green with the line pointing down the start line I've read in the putt. Then, I have another guide line to help me when I take my stance. The line on the ball also matches up to the guide line etched on the top of my putter.

When you're setting your feet, don't look down at the ball. Look at the spot you've picked as the apex of the break. Use the line on the ball as confirmation of your read.

When I set up behind the ball, I get into my stance and put my right hand on the club first, all while looking at my target. I keep looking at the target until I set my left-hand grip, and I only look down at the ball when I'm ready to hit the putt.

LEAVE

Leave is a more sophisticated skill than green reading, because it incorporates both reading and strategy. You might know that a putt breaks from left to right, or that it's uphill, but understanding leave means you've determined the best place to leave the ball for an easy second putt, should you miss. The skill is a lot like the one a good pool player has—seeing the next shot.

We can talk about how putts move from left to right—and we did, back in the chapter about lag putting—but I want you to understand that speed and leave are much more important than the basic read. I see players at every level giving themselves a lot of problems because they hit a putt too hard or too soft and leave a difficult second putt. Those kinds of problems hurt your score a lot more than seeing too little or too much break in a twenty- or thirty-footer—a putt the odds say you probably won't make very often anyway. If all you do is dial in your speed and get a sense for the "safe" place to leave your first putt, you can go from a 20-handicap to a 15 in the course of a week. Without changing a thing about your swing. It's that important.

Tour players are very good about understanding when to be aggressive with a putt and when to be conservative. They are conservative when the penalty for missing is severe. For example, if I have a putt that is downhill and fast, I know that the last thing I want is to leave it short, where I have another delicate, fast downhill putt. So my mistake, if I miss, is to hit that putt past the hole.

The average player usually does the opposite. He babies the putt because of how afraid he is of the speed, and he's then in three-putt position.

Generally speaking, you're trying to lag your long putts onto the same tier as the flag, and in position to have an uphill putt with as little break as possible. Personally, I'd rather be left with four or five feet straight up a hill than a putt half that distance downhill with some break. And if I have a big breaking putt—say, a twenty-footer with five feet of break—my tendency is to make my mistake on the low side, below the hole, and slightly long, so I can hit the next putt uphill. If I played that putt with too much break and with too little speed, I'd be above the hole, putting downhill.

The opposite, of course, is also true. If you're ten feet away and below the hole, you can be more aggressive with your stroke on that uphill putt. Giving it more speed also lets you play a straighter line with less break, if that's what you prefer. Personally, I like to follow Harvey Penick's classic advice: Give luck a chance. A ball that's dying close to the hole has a chance to drop in even if it's slightly off line. If you charge it to the hole, you're usually going to lip out if you're slightly off line.

PRESSURE

Golf isn't played on the practice green. In real life, you're standing over a putt that has consequences—beating your career-best score, a $3 Nassau with your friend, or winning a match in the club championship. Learning to deal with those pressure situations on the green is a big part of a successful putting strategy.

By now I've given you a number of questions to ask yourself around the green. And it's a simple thing to add one more. You need to be conscious of when you're tense and nervous, and ask yourself what that tends to do to your putting stroke.

Most pressure putts get missed short of the hole, not long. When the heat turns up, your tension level rises and you hold on to the putter much more tightly. When everything is clenched, your muscles don't transmit as much energy to the putterhead. If you're aware of this, you can account for it and use a little more force on your putts.

When I was at my best in tournament play, it wasn't because I didn't get nervous. It happened because I followed my putting checklist the same way under pressure as I did back on the practice green, when the heat wasn't on yet.

I had a pre-putt process that was designed to get me thinking about my routine and my stroke, not about making the putt. I wanted to be process oriented, not results oriented. If I did my job with my preparation—asking all the questions—and made my stroke, the results would take care of themselves.

First, I committed to the putt I wanted to hit—lagging it versus trying to make it—which determined the line I would pick. Then I held the putter with the my right hand and stood behind the ball, facing the starting point of the line I picked, and took a deep breath and let it out, to release tension. Then I walked in and took a practice stroke, visualized my line, and saw the ball rolling into the cup. Next I plugged in the swing thought that I was using for the day—say, letting my forearms release. Then I let it go.

The way I judged my result was not based on whether or not the ball went in the hole. It was based on whether or not I committed myself to the shot and executed my routine. I found that focusing hard on the routine helped me deal with the nervousness. And if I executed my routine, it took away some of the disappointment when I missed an important putt. Not all of it, of course. But it's easier to accept missing when you feel like you did all you could to try to make it. Sometimes the ball just hits a bump and kicks off line. And sometimes you just aren't as sharp. You can't beat yourself up about that.

Believe it or not, in the end, the way you make more putts is by not "trying" to make more putts. Control the things you can control—information, preparation, and your stroke—and realize that you don't control the rest. If you can stop focusing on the hole and trust this question-asking process (and the stroke we worked on in Chapter 3), you're going to make more putts in the end. I realize that's a tough thing to accept, but it's true.

When I talk about this concept at an outing, people always ask me how I judged my play if it wasn't necessarily about how many putts I made. It's simple. Remember the scorecard tabs I showed you in Chapter 1? For every tournament round, I keep track of how many shots I make using my full routine and giving my best effort. Sometimes, I'll manage to stay focused on most of my shots but still shoot 73—and that's OK. Other times, I may shoot 68 or 69, but I'll still know that I left a lot of shots out there because I wasn't as successful with my routine. And I'll be disappointed.

A good example of this is the round where I set the PGA Tour record for the fewest putts for nine holes—six, at the Air Canada Classic in 2002. Everybody talks about that round as a great putting round, but the record came because I missed a lot of greens, chipped in twice, holed a bunker shot and chipped it close the rest of the time. So I might have been satisfied with my short game that day, but I wasn't necessarily thrilled with how I was playing in general. By following what I've been talking about here, you can develop your sense of "good" and "bad" in your own game to a much more sophisticated degree.

Chapter 8

TOUR SCHOOL

· ·

T he strategies and techniques we've been talking about throughout this book are the same for every player. We're all dealing with the same basic physics, right?

But I'm sure you won't be surprised to hear that my responsibilities when I'm conducting a two-hour clinic with a group of good amateur players are a little different than they would be when I'm working with Sergio Garcia in a session at Grayhawk during the off-season.

First of all, the stakes are a little different. There's no doubt that it's very important to me that the amateur players in a clinic get better by the end of the day—just like I want you to get to the end of this book with some real pieces of advice to improve your short game. But the stakes are way higher with a tour player, because there's much more of a penalty if I give them something that makes them worse—for whatever reason.

A tour player's livelihood depends on being able to get the ball in the hole—and on getting and using the right advice for his or her game. Tiger Woods and Sergio Garcia aren't going to starve to death if they can't play golf anymore, but they have a lot riding on being able to continue to play at a high level. And in the next couple of tiers of players, you're talking about people who are on the edge of being able to make a living by playing, or else finding some other line of work.

I take my responsibilities as a teacher very seriously, but especially so when it comes to the people who have so much on the line.

The tour players who come to see me fall into two general categories. The first group is made up of players who are in a crisis. They've had a string of really poor results, and they feel like they can't trust what has gotten them to this point. Or they're finding that they can't be competitive because they're missing some piece of the short game. Maybe it's a European player who wants to get better at playing the lofted shots you need on the American tour. Or a Champions Tour guy who just isn't getting enough out of his ball-striking. Or an LPGA player who has never really had any guidance about her putting stroke, and now that she's really struggling, she doesn't know what to try.

The second group is made up of players who feel good about what they're doing but want another set of eyes to give them some feedback. With those players, I'm poking around trying to understand what they need from me. Are they looking for somebody to confirm for them that they're doing what they think they're doing—right or wrong? Do they want advice about what changes I believe would make them better? I'm trying to assess how realistically they see their own situation, and how open they are to hearing new information.

Regardless of what group you're talking about, though, the thing that stands out is the talent. The men and women playing professional golf have incredible talent. You're talking about people who can immediately pick up the subtlety of what I'm trying to share, start to incorporate it within two or three shots, and use it in tournament play later that week, or for sure within a week or two.

Some players stand out even in that group—players you dream

about teaching because there's no limit to what they can do. Sergio Garcia is a player with this sort of extreme talent. He's right up there with Tiger Woods as the best pure ballstriker on the planet, and he has exquisite control over the ball in his long game. He can stand up on the tee and feel the shot he needs—say, a low, penetrating draw with the driver—and execute it as if it was second nature.

I had seen how great he was with his long game, and that he had some struggles with his putter, so when the chance came to help him, I was very excited—and, to be honest, a little nervous. I always am when it comes to working with tour players. I want to help you as much as I want to help Sergio, but Sergio's livelihood depends on his golf game. I can't just throw a bunch of suggestions out and hope that one of them works, because there's a real possibility that not only would I fail to help him improve, but I might actually make him worse.

The other piece of the puzzle to consider was Sergio's background in receiving instruction. At the tour level, players can work with any teacher they like—literally. Walk down the range at any event and you can find a dozen instructors, and another fifty are just a phone call or text message away. The challenge for the player is picking the right teacher and getting a consistent message that's compatible with the way he plays and thinks. Sergio was very fortunate because he decided early on that he was going to trust his dad, Victor, with his golf swing. He always knew that he would have someone who was looking out for his best interests—both on and off the course.

So when Billy Foster, one of Sergio's caddies (he alternates between two during the season), texted me about helping Sergio during the winter before the 2008 season, I knew I was going to have to be careful about my approach. I knew that Sergio would probably be skeptical at the start—and rightfully so. I have caddies, wives, and agents calling me pretty regularly about potentially helping a player, but in my experience, it never works out unless the player buys in and wants the help. I wanted Sergio to see what I was about and to decide for himself if I could help him—and whether the things I shared with him were going to work within the framework of his dad's supervision.

We met for the first time at the Match Play in Tucson, and I did what I do every time I see a potential student for the first time. I watched Sergio hit a few putts, and then I asked him about what he was trying to do, and what his frustrations were about his putting. He said his putting stats looked okay, but when he had a bad day, he didn't know why, and he didn't know how to fix it. He was using a belly putter because he felt more comfortable with it, but it wasn't something he wanted to keep doing. He said he felt lost, and he didn't know what to work on. When it came to his stroke, he said that when he had a long putt, his overriding thought was, "How am I going to get the ball all the way to the hole?"

In the course of a dozen putts or so, I could see in some of his basic fundamentals why he was having trouble with his putting. His ball position was too far forward. From there, the tendency is to hit pulls. When that happens, a player subconsciously leaves the face open to compensate. Also, when the ball is too far forward, the shaft tends to lean back, away from the target, and you catch the ball too much on the upswing. The bottom of the putter hits the top of the ball, and that thin contact encourages you to use more "hit" with the hands to compensate for the loss of energy.

All of those compensations translated into non-solid contact. Without even considering his stroke, we made some setup adjustments that helped him hit the ball in the center of the putterface. We moved his ball position to the center and adjusted his grip position at address a full two inches forward, toward the target—a big change. Once he was making solid contact, he was on the road back to using his incredible talent to hole putts—within a half hour. And holing putts is what makes these players geniuses. They have a great sense for it. My job is to help them make solid contact, and the talent takes over from there. And when it comes to talent, Sergio has as much as you could ever dream of. He didn't need a hot putter to win tournaments. He just needed to avoid putting badly.

By the end of that first session, Sergio said he felt much more comfortable with his putter. The comment that resonated the most with me was when he said his putting felt like it did when he was a kid. That was music to my ears, because my goal was to help him unlock that genius that is so obviously in him.

Of course, feeling more comfortable and seeing results are related, but they don't always go together. What matters in the end is that you can make a good stroke when the heat turns up the highest. I know Sergio would have liked to have had a better result at the PGA Championship—where he finished second to Padraig Harrington—but he was right there in contention in a lot of big tournaments throughout 2008, and he didn't feel like his putter let him down. I don't see him make many bad strokes these days.

One of the most interesting elements of Sergio's game emerged as we spent more time working on his putting. The putting was definitely getting better—he won the Players Championship after we had been working together for about two months—so we started talking a little bit about the rest of his short game.

Sergio has an incredible pair of hands, and he has hit some spectacular short game shots over the course of his career. Like Seve Ballesteros and Jose Maria Olazabal, a couple of Spanish legends who came before him, Sergio can see a shot where most players would just see trouble, and if he can visualize it, he can execute it.

The interesting thing I noticed was that he was pretty ordinary on "ordinary" shots—basic chip shots and pitch shots. That was something I had heard from his caddies, and it was really true. And believe it or not, that's pretty common with world-class players. When a player has one choice—say, a flop shot out of deep grass—he can "see" it right away. When he has lots of choices, it becomes harder. That's something we talked a little bit about in Chapter 4, in the section about playing a shot from rough close to the hole.

Sergio's problem on chips and pitches was that the thing that makes him such a great ballstriker in his long game—the huge lag he has during the downswing—hurt his short game. On a lot of short game shots, it's important for the club to be vertical at impact. With Sergio's lag, his hands were coming through really early and the club was trailing behind. This made it hard for him to expose the bounce on the bottom of his wedges. Essentially, he was digging the leading edge of the club into the ground, instead of skipping his club through the grass at impact. He's a super talented guy, so he could get by with his touch and feel, but he hit too many poor chips for a guy with his talent. He wasn't making it as easy as he could for himself.

As I said before, if you're going to make changes in a tour player's short game, you have to be careful about how you do it. It's a delicate, deliberate process, because the player has to feel comfortable with what he's taking out into competition.

At the Players Championship in 2008, we worked on a low pitch shot where he turned his left hand down, covered the ball, and let it chase onto the green. Like I do, he preferred to play most of his shots around the green with his lofted wedge—as opposed to using a pitching wedge or an 8-iron for a running shot. But he hadn't learned to hit the running shot with his wedge without putting a lot of backspin on the ball. Because of all the backspin his technique caused, he needed to play a shot that landed nearer the hole and checked up. That made it hard for him to judge shots that had to land before they reached the putting green. Once he learned to hit that running shot without backspin, he had the option of playing more shots. For example, he could run the ball through the fringe to a pin on the front of the green without worrying about the ball getting caught up in the grass. So it was really fun to see him go out and not only use that shot on the 18th hole to get up and down, but to win the tournament, too.

Through that summer, he really started letting the club release in his pitching and chipping game, and he hit some beautiful shots. He played really well at the PGA Championship, where he was a putt or two away from winning, and he looked solid throughout the FedEx events at the end of the season.

All along, Sergio has been very open to listening, trying, and learning. He wants to get better so badly, and that's very rewarding for a teacher. He's got some work left to do to get his basic shots more fundamentally sound, but he is well on his way. With his talent, when he has confidence on and around the greens, the sky is literally the limit, and I'm enjoying helping him get there.

So much of a tour player's improvement depends upon whether he can identify the piece of his game that's holding him back and do what it takes to improve it. And not only that, he has to be able to improve this one piece without diminishing the other parts of his game. I know this firsthand: I spent my playing career trying to improve my long game, and I worked on it to the point that it hurt the things I was good at, namely putting and chipping.

Two other players I've been working with, Dudley Hart on the PGA Tour and Paige MacKenzie on the LPGA Tour, have gone through the same thing.

Dudley's dad was a longtime teaching professional, and Dudley, like Sergio, had learned from his dad that you should retain the lag in your wrists for as long as possible. And also like Sergio, Dudley struggled to hit his short sand wedge shots because he never let the clubhead release. As I said, these guys are talented. So Dudley could work around his problem and hit some decent ones, but he wasn't as consistent as he would have liked. Sometimes, he'd hold off his release and cut across the ball, dumping a shot short. Other times, he'd release the club and hit a hot one too long.

To Dudley's credit, he saw that his short game was holding him back, and he went looking for ways to improve his technique that would help him shoot better scores. We spent a lot of time working on getting his left wrist more relaxed and the club less shut down through impact. And he struggled with it at first, because it was counter to what he was doing on every full swing. I told Dudley about a lesson I had given a sixty-four-year-old guy with the same problem. That guy's teacher had told him to "hold the angle" on every shot, and pull the grip as fast as he could. Of course, every time he did that on a pitch or a chip, he hit it thin or skulled it. During our first lesson together, I used the same drill we talked about in Chapter 4. I asked him to simply let the clubhead fall to the ground and add a little bit of turn to it.

Dudley has great hands, and as soon as he let that clubhead fall, he hit nice shots right away. With almost no effort, the ball just popped up into the air nicely. The challenge for any player, PGA Tour or otherwise, is not just to understand the change in technique, but to learn a new feel. Dudley's feel went from being in really firm, tight control of the grip and holding it in place as he swung to letting the clubhead respond to centrifugal force on its own, without any interference from his hands. He basically just started holding on lightly and letting gravity do the work.

The more you can get out of the way of physics—gravity, centrifugal force—and your own talent, the better you're going to be in your short game and putting. That's true for the average player, and it's even more important when you have a ton of athletic ability.

I got a call from Paige MacKenzie early in the 2008 season for some putting help. I knew her record—she was a fantastic college player who had won a bunch of tournaments at the University of Washington before turning pro in 2006—but I had never seen her play. She's one of the best athletes on the LPGA, and she has a strong all-around game. But when I watched her putt for the first time, on the practice green at the McDonald's LPGA Championship, I saw a player fighting against her own talent.

It wasn't that she was standing over those putts without any idea about what she wanted to do. She had been taught to keep her arms "connected" to her body and to use the big muscles to putt, and she was following those directions well. But she had a wide stance, and she locked her elbows in a stiff, straight position. She was trying to take the putter straight back and move it straight toward the target. So the face of the putter was closing on the way back, and opening on the way through.

Putting had become a super mechanical process for her, and she wasn't getting any of the benefit of her natural athleticism. The first thing I did with her was to find a spot fifty feet from the hole on the practice green and ask her to hit some putts to it with just her right hand. Once she stopped thinking so hard about keeping her arms locked and moving the putter back and through on a straight line and instead just concentrated on hitting the ball, she started releasing the putterhead. She had to, it was the only way to get the ball across the green and near the hole.

The first few putts were awkward and wristy, but after a few minutes, her athleticism came through and she started consistently rolling the ball up in a nice circle three or four feet around the hole. Once I got her to accept that swinging the putter on an arc and letting it release was the best way to unlock her talent, she was just a few adjustments in her setup away from getting much better.

The "liberation" of Paige's putting stroke is something I see a lot with players who have some experience—from 10-handicappers to tour players. When I'm working with somebody like Paige who has had some layers of instruction, I definitely don't want to add things to what they already do with the putter. I'm trying to peel things away. I'm trying to make the stroke as simple and efficient as possible.

Another good example of simplifying a player's game comes from the work Troy Matteson and I have done together. Troy is a guy who has dominated at every level. He was a great college player—he won the 2002 NCAA Championship when he was at Georgia Tech—and he won pretty quickly when he came out on both the Nationwide and PGA Tours.

Troy is a super-smart guy—an engineering major—who had pretty much been self-taught. He asked me to take a look at his short game in mid-2008. The particular shot that gave him problems was the high, soft pitch. Troy's method was a classic example of making a shot much harder than it needed to be. His backswing went up and outside the plane, and his clubface was completely closed. I explained to him that he had the face pointed down and the bounce on the club pointed up—the exact opposite of the easy way to make the club work.

Troy is so talented that he could get away with poor technique a lot of the time. But at his level, those soft pitch shots should really be easy plays. He should be looking to hit them right by the hole, not using every ounce of his skill just to pull them off.

Over the course of a month, he made a dramatic change in his technique. His clubhead in the backswing path ended up in a position a foot and a half flatter—a huge difference on such a small swing. It clicked in for him at the John Deere, when he had a delicate shot on the 9th hole that previously would have given him a lot of anxiety. He committed to using the new method, and the shot came out perfectly. He got results under pressure with it, and that's all that matters to a tour player.

Kevin Streelman is another one of those players I was talking about who is right on the edge of breaking through. And his results over the last few years show how fine the line is between feeling good about what you're doing and making a living and struggling and going home early.

We first met early in 2007, and Kevin took some of the things we talked about and used them to dominate the Gateway Tour that season, winning three times. At the end of the season, he made it through all three stages of PGA Tour Qualifying School—some of the most intense pressure you'll find on a golf course—to earn his tour card for 2008.

Kevin is like a lot of players—it's easy for him to slide a little bit out of whack with his fundamentals. It doesn't take him long to get back to them, but he needs a second set of eyes and some tweaks.

In 2008, he had just come off missing the cut at the Bob Hope, and he and I got together early the week of the Buick Invitational in San Diego. Kevin's tendency is to let his putting alignment drift, and to let his hands get too low or too high. It throws his stroke completely out of whack, and he starts pushing or pulling putts to try to get them back on the right line. That's a recipe for some seriously inconsistent putting. When I saw him in San Diego, we had a pretty straightforward session. It was simply a matter of getting him lined up the right way again, with his hands in a more neutral position. He could feel it click in right away.

He was one of the last alternates to get in the field there, and sure enough, he was playing with Tiger Woods late in the day on Saturday. He faltered on the weekend, but he got a lot of great experience, and he got to test the things he was working on under fire.

I saw Kevin again the week of the U.S. Open, and we had a similar session where we tweaked some of his alignments. He went out and led the Open after the first round. The next step, obviously, was for him to put together four rounds in a week and really make a good check. It came together for him the next week, at the Travelers Championship in Hartford, where he shot 62-63 on Friday and Saturday and ended up finishing 10th. The next week, at the Buick Open in Flint, he shot four rounds of 70 or better to end up 12th.

He finished out his season by breaking into the top ten three different times. At the Barclays, he tied for fourth and made a huge check, $290,000, to basically sew up his tour card for the season. Then, at Disney in the last event of the season, he made nine birdies in the first round to shoot 64, and played a great finishing round on Sunday—a bogey-free 68—to tie for 6th.

People don't realize how difficult it is for a PGA Tour rookie to go out and play a season on courses he's seeing for the first time, against players with way more tournament experience and more experience on the particular courses on the schedule. For most players not named Tiger Woods, rookie year is mostly about surviving and learning how to be a professional.

Kevin certainly did a lot of learning, but he always kept his composure, and he was able to put what he learned into play quickly. He earned $1.4 million and finished 78th in money—a fantastic season for a rookie.

The lesson you can learn from this is to find a local teacher or a golf-savvy buddy you trust and ask him or her to check you out when you feel like you're playing well. Once they know what you look like when you're playing well, they should be able to give you some valuable feedback when you're struggling—that tweak helped Kevin go from missing cuts to making a million bucks. The goal is finding what "good" looks like for you, and more importantly, being able to identify "good" when you—or a friend—sees it.

My own golf-savvy buddy turned out to be my wife, Elayna. I was midway through a round in a pro-am event at Pebble Beach that had the notable advantage of allowing wives to ride along in the cart. Elayna asked if my putter was supposed to have the angle to it that it did. Now, that advice could mean a million things, but I asked her if she meant that I looked like I was standing too far away from the ball. She said yes, and it clicked for me that my posture was off. I was reaching for the ball, and the toe of the putter was a little bit off the ground in my address position. I was pulling my putts. After adjusting my setup, I made five birdies in the last ten holes, and it was all because of a simple observation from my wife, who probably hasn't seen me putt a dozen balls in the last five years. She just knew I didn't look the way I usually look.

It's a good thing Elayna gets so much joy out of being home with our kids in Scottsdale. Otherwise, she might bump me out of some teaching assignments!

Chapter 9

INSIDE THE SHOTMAKER'S BAG

· ·

The strategies and techniques we've been talking about for the last eight chapters work no matter what kind of clubs you have in your bag. If you practice these things, you're going to get better.

That said, if you use equipment that fits your body, fits your stroke, and complements the style of short game swing and putting stroke I teach, you're going to improve even more. I've seen it happen over and over again—sometimes in a matter of minutes. I'll be working with a tour player who doesn't like the way his putts are rolling, and I'll take a look at his putter. He might be using a Ping Anser–style putter with a thin neck that's bent so that the putter has no loft. After a simple adjustment to the putter, he's back rolling the ball great again.

Or maybe a player has wedges that are too close together in loft. So she has two clubs that work great on the same shot, and she might be missing a club that would work great on a different shot she sees six or seven times in a round. Again, that's a simple matter of switching out some wedges.

The equipment part of scoring is just another element of strategy you can work to your benefit. And with so many different golf shops and equipment manufacturers making it easier than ever to not only get measured for the right gear but to get very individualized stuff, there's no excuse not to take advantage. Let's start by talking about set makeup.

I break down the clubs you need into two categories: the traveling set (the fourteen clubs you have in your bag most of the time), and the specialized tools (hybrids and wedges for non-standard conditions).

Let's start with the basics. In a standard set configuration, you'd have a driver and a 3-wood separated by at least 4 degrees of loft (say, 11 degrees for the driver and 16 for the 3-wood), a 5-wood, two hybrids (replacing the 3- and 4-irons in your set), five irons, three wedges, and a putter. Honestly, it doesn't matter what the numbers say on the bottoms of your irons. What you really need is a regular interval of distance between the longest iron in your bag and the shortest. If your 5-iron goes 180 yards and your gap wedge goes 100, you want to be able to hit those other six clubs at regular distance intervals, without any big gaps. For example, if you hit that 5-iron 180, the 6-iron 175, and the 7-iron 150, you have a big gap where you won't be able to hit a comfortable, full shot. You would need to have the 6-iron bent so that it fit more in the middle of that gap.

Having the right loft gaps is even more important when it comes to wedges. If you go from a 46-degree pitching wedge to a 60-degree lob wedge, you're not giving yourself enough flexibility with your short game. In other words, you're going to have to manufacture many more shots than are necessary, rather than simply hitting them with a pretty standard swing. That spacing between your clubs should go through the set—you should have regular yardage gaps between your clubs, so that you can hit the widest variety of shots with a "standard" swing.

A big part of the yardage gap conversation is the kind of player you are—regardless of your handicap. If you hit it far, say 265 yards or more off the tee (on a 6,500-yard course), you're probably better off with four wedges—pitching wedge (46 degrees), gap (50), sand wedge (55 or 56), and L wedge (58 or 60). If you're a shorter hitter, an extra fairway wood or hybrid is probably going to make more sense—it'll give you more help reaching the green. If you're a longer hitter, you're going to have more shots to hit with the short clubs. If you're a shorter hitter, you're going to have more long shots. Your set makeup should reflect that.

In the standard wedge configuration, you need to be very sensitive to bounce angle, as well. A club's bounce is the amount of metal it has hanging below the leading edge to help it skip through sand or grass. It is measured in degrees—a higher number means more bounce, or more skip versus dig. If you look on the bottom of most decent wedges, you'll see a rating for both loft (56 degrees, 58 degrees, etc.) and bounce (4 degrees, 8 degrees, etc.). If you're a 15-handicapper or higher, you want your main short game wedge to have 58 degrees of loft and at least 10 degrees of bounce. That extra bounce is going to help you skip the club through the sand and rough and hit more consistent shots. The rest of your wedges should have at least eight degrees of bounce. If you're a better player, you can get away with less bounce on the club, because you can move the shaft forward or backward to create more or less loft and bounce.

We've talked about techniques like this one that make you less reliant on technology, but the technology certainly does help, especially when you're a higher handicapper.

Here's what I'm carrying in my bag right now:

Driver, 7.5 degrees loft, 260 carry
3-wood, 13 degrees loft, 230 carry
2-hybrid, 17 degrees, 215 carry
3-hybrid, 21 degrees, 200 carry
4-iron, 190 carry
5-iron, 180 carry
6-iron, 170 carry

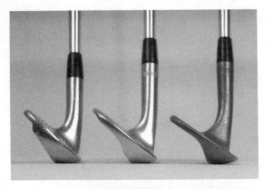

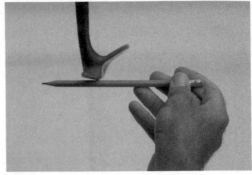

(ABOVE LEFT) I carry three wedges (left to right): a 48-degree pitching wedge, a 52-degree gap wedge with 10 degrees of bounce, and a 58--degree sand wedge with 12 degrees of bounce. I use the 58-degree for most of my short game shots.

(ABOVE RIGHT) Bounce is the measurement of the amount of metal that hangs below the leading edge of the clubface. A wedge with more bounce (say, 12 degrees, like my sand wedge) has more metal hanging below the leading edge.

(LEFT) I had bounce material from the heel and toe of my sand wedge shaved down—this allows me to hit different kinds of shots by opening or closing the clubface. For example, if I were playing a shot from a very firm lie, I could open the club slightly so that it rested more on the heel, where there is less bounce material. This would prevent the club from skipping off the hard ground so much through impact.

....

7-iron, 155 carry

8-iron, 140 carry

9-iron, 130 carry

PW, 48 degrees, 120 carry

GW, 52 degrees, 10 degrees bounce, 105 carry

SW, 58 degrees, 12 degrees bounce, 85 carry
Putter, 5 degrees loft

I like the extra hybrid versus a 5-wood because I can use the hybrid more easily from the rough, and it plays more like an iron on par-3 tee shots. It's also easier to curve left or right. You might pick a 5-wood instead, or drop the 2-hybrid and carry a lob wedge to make it easier to hit higher shots. If I need to play something higher, I shift the grip on my sand wedge back at setup to increase the effective loft and play the shot that way. The important thing is to have a combination that feels comfortable for you.

Once you have your basic configuration down, you might want to add a few extra clubs that stay in the garage until you need them. If you're the longer hitter I talked about, you might want an extra hybrid with some loft for when you're playing an exceptionally long course (where you're going to need more choices for long approach shots), or for when you're playing a really tight course, where a hybrid or a 5-wood might be a smarter, more accurate choice off the tee. Switching out for a hybrid is also a good idea in wet conditions, when a longer iron's sharper leading edge might get bogged down in the wet turf. The hybrid glides over the top like a fairway wood.

In terms of wedges, I like matching sets, because the specs are complementary to start with, which saves a lot of bending and measuring to make sure the gaps are correct. A 58-degree wedge from one company might not perform like a 58-degree from a different company. You might have a 56-degree from one company and a 60-degree from the other that are fundamentally the same. If both are in your bag, you're wasting a slot for a different club that could help you out of a trouble spot.

I carry a 58-degree wedge that serves as my main short game club. I also have an identical backup that was built at the same time, so I can go back home and get an exact copy if the airline loses my bag or something like that. Touch and feel are sensitive things, especially with wedges. Knowing you have another club at home that is built the same is certainly comforting.

Players often ask me if they should get different wedges for different course conditions—like the hard and dry fairways of midsummer versus the lush, wet turf of spring. On tour, most players only switch the bounce characteristics of their wedges when the conditions are dramatically different. Bob Vokey gets a lot of requests for wedges with less bounce leading up to the British Open, because the ground is hard and the grass is thin. There, the club skips more abruptly if it hits the ground, so having less bounce feels and plays more normal for these extreme conditions.

If you buy a set of wedges you're comfortable with and learn how to hit them, you're going to be OK for virtually any conditions. Another way I have more flexibility built into my clubs is through the grind on the bounce of my sand wedge. My club has more bounce material on the toe and less on the heel, so I can change how I set the club on the ground for different conditions. At one point, I would have Mr. Vokey put a special grind on the heel of my 58-degree wedge, but Titleist has now released what's called the "M Grind"—which is basically the same as what I have.

When it comes to putters, fitting is just as important, but there's a little more art to the process, too. Unfortunately, a lot of players use a putter they got as a pro-am gift, inherited from a friend, or bought off the rack. What I often see in this circumstance is that the player adjusts his setup and stroke to fit the putter, and then can't understand why the club isn't performing the way he would like. It always works better to fit the equipment to the player, not the other way around.

Picking a putter is a lot like picking a pair of shoes. When I buy shoes, I agonize over the purchase because I've got narrow feet, which makes it hard for me to find ones that feel great. But when I find a pair that I like, I take care of them and keep them for years. A good putter is the same way. The club needs to fit, it needs to feel comfortable, and it has to look good to your eye. The four measurements that go into putter fitting are length, lie angle, loft, and weight.

The putters that I fit for people range in length from 31 to 37 inches. Most fall in the 34- to 35-inch range. If your putter is too short, you'll tend to keep your arms too straight and your elbows locked—which creates a rigid putting stroke. You'll also tend to stand too close to the ball, which may put your eyes outside the ball line. If the putter is too long—which happens a lot with women and children—you'll tend to stand too upright at address, get too far away from the ball, and possibly bend your elbows too much.

The way to find the correct length of putter is pretty straightforward. Once you get into a comfortable setup position, the putter has to be long enough to create a slight bend in your elbows while they lie relaxed against your sides. The last major factor is the position of your eyes relative to the target line. I prefer them to be between one and three inches inside the ball at setup. (By "comfortable setup," I mean that I'd like you to have a narrow stance, with your upper body tilted toward the ball from the hips and a fairly straight spine. Your arms need to hang down tension-free from your shoulders, and they should remain next to your sides, with the elbow joints soft, not extended.) When your eyes are just inside the ball line, the normal distance between your toes and the ball is two or two and a half putterheads.

Lie angle and loft are the next two measurements I'd check if I were fitting you for a new putter. The correct lie angle—the angle between the sole of the putter and the shaft—is pretty simple to find. You need to have your forearms and shaft on the same plane when you're looking from behind, down the target line. Once you're in this position, the lie angle is correct when your putter is flat on the ground. Of the students I see who aren't fit correctly, most have a putter that is too upright. This promotes a tendency to set up with the hands too high, or to start putts to the left. Once you see putts going to the left like that, you're going to start holding the face open to prevent it. That's a bad compensation. Standard putters come with about 71 degrees of lie angle. Most players I fit leave with a lie angle of around 69 degrees—noticeably flatter than "standard."

As for loft, you might wonder why it's even an issue on a putter. Putters have loft because the ball sits down slightly in the turf, not like it would on a hard surface like a tabletop. You need some loft to be able to get the ball out of that depression and rolling on its way. If you don't have enough loft on your putter at impact, you'll hit the ball into the side of its depression, causing it to lose speed and bounce off line. In other words, you could be missing more than your share of putts because the loft on your putter is off by two or three degrees. It's that important.

Most of my students show up with putters that have 2 to 4 degrees of loft. Several variables come into play for a correct loft fit. First, I believe you need 3 degrees of loft at impact on a normal fifteen-footer to get your best roll. I believe good putters will slightly change the loft at impact depending on how hard they need to hit the putt to get to the hole. On a short putt, I tend to have true loft at impact. From fifteen to twenty feet, I deloft slightly, and on a long putt I deloft considerably. These subtle changes are what cause the ball to leave my putter face with a good roll, rather than a lot of hops and bounces.

A putter usually comes from the factory with 2 degrees of loft. I don't think that's enough to roll the ball consistently well. I prefer a little more—like 5 degrees—because of the way it affects how a player sets up to the putt. If a player is using a putter with less than the proper amount of loft, he or she tends to shift the shaft backward, away from the target, at address, in a subconscious effort to get the ball rolling. That promotes a hand flip and thin contact. Also, if you're playing most of your golf in one area, and your greens are slow and bumpy, you'll probably want even more loft, like 6 degrees.

The art of putter fitting comes in when you start talking about the weight of the club. My preference is a putter that has a swingweight similar to my irons, which is D-2. It is very common today for players to prefer slightly heavier putters that swing at D-6 or D-8, and most standard putters come in this weight. This is something you'll have to experiment with. Just keep in mind that swingweight is going to have a significant impact on your tempo and feel. A heavier putter wants to move on a longer, slower arc, while a lighter putter is better for a faster, more aggressive stroke. My advice about your stroke doesn't change based on how heavy your putter is, but the weight of the putter you pick should match your tempo and stroke characteristics.

The shape of the putter head you pick is a personal preference. I've been using putters with the same look for twenty-five years. I use a modified Scotty Cameron Newport model now, and I've always used a putter with that head style. I would say that if you ever putted great with a putter in the past, go back and find it. At least get it measured, so you can understand why it felt so good.

Now, shape is a personal preference, but understand that some aspects of how a putter is designed will impact how you swing it. Putters are built with different kinds of weight distribution— primarily based on whether they're center-shafted or heel-shafted. Some are "face-balanced," which means that if you balance the putter shaft on your finger, the face points straight up—a center-shafted design. A face-balanced putter wants to travel in a straight line—not on a gentle arc like I teach.

If a putter has a shaft that enters the head toward the heel, the toe will hang down when you balance it on your finger. My preference is for the toe to hang at about 45 degrees. That amount of toe hang seems to work best with the stroke I teach. The more toe hang you use, the more the club will help you swing on an arc. Of course, you can also overcook that and have a putter that causes you to rotate the face too much.

What happens if you use a face-balanced putter and swing on an arc? You'd have to consciously make the putter swing on that arc with extra forearm rotation, rather than having it happen naturally. A face-balanced putter will travel where you send it, while a putter with toe hang will move naturally on the curve. Can you put well enough using what I teach you and a face-balanced putter? Sure. But I think you should make the stroke as easy and nonconscious as possible. When Sergio Garcia and I first met, he came out with a face-balanced putter. After about thirty minutes of work, he went straight to the equipment truck and got a new putter, and he's never looked back.

Also, as you become a better putter, you'll notice that you're getting a lot more feedback from your hands and the putter-head. You'll start to feel when you just missed the sweet spot on the putterface. Personally, I like to know when I'm hitting it solid, and that feedback is an important part of the game for me. I think you get more feedback from a putter with toe hang than you do with a face-balanced model.

I even took it a step further with my putter. I cut a channel in the sole of my putter so I could hear a solid strike. I happen to like a crisper, louder sound. Whatever sound your putter makes, you need to be able to identify it when you make good contact. You have to know the difference between solid contact and thin contact, which occurs when the bottom half of the putterface makes contact with the middle of the ball. If you're lifting up or flipping the putter out in front of your hands before impact, you're probably hitting almost every putt thin. The putt doesn't have the same energy it would have if you hit it solidly. A tell-tale sign is that every once in awhile you'll hit the ball way past the hole. You get used to not hitting it solidly, and when you do catch one right, it goes way too far.

I can't stress enough the importance of using equipment that fits you. You'll solve a lot of your stroke problems with that one step—before you even make any changes in your swing fundamentals. I've given hundreds of lessons where a player will hit a half dozen putts on the practice green and I'll immediately spot a glaring equipment-based reason why the ball isn't rolling nicely. Then it's just a matter of making some equipment adjustments, such as bending the putter. A good fitter's eye will help, and fitters also have a lot more technology at their disposal now.

I'm using a machine called the SAM PuttLab in both my teaching and putter fitting, and the information I can get from it is just incredible. I attach an ultrasound wand to the shaft of the student's putter, and the machine registers all of the putter's movements to the smallest degree, and in three dimensions. In a series of easy-to-read graphics, I can see the path the putter is taking, where the face is at impact (or at any other point in the stroke), and the rhythm and length of the stroke. It also shows how consistently you make impact on the same spot on the putterface.

With so much specific information, it's easy to isolate specific issues in the stroke itself, or to compare different putters to see which one produces the best roll. With the tour players I teach, I record their strokes when we first start working together, and then when they feel like they're really putting well. The graphs are a great way to show the differences and improvements, and the graph of the good stroke is a great baseline to use going forward. Then, when the player tells me he's struggling with his stroke, I can watch for certain things, and then confirm the diagnosis on the machine. There's something about seeing the numbers in full color on the laptop screen that adds to the authority of what a teacher can say with words or demonstration. The PuttLab software comes with a database of measurements of hundreds of the best putting strokes in golf, so you can go through and check your own stroke for, say, face rotation though impact and measure it against what Tiger Woods or Brad Faxon does.

All of this information—from the stuff about set makeup earlier in this chapter to all the technology you can now use for putter fitting—might seem like a lot to digest, but these are all factors that can be controlled before you start your stroke. And it's all so easy to access—either through the teaching pro at your club or one of the big golf retailers. Take advantage of it. It's a quick way to cut shots from your score.

Chapter 10
QUICK REFERENCE GUIDE

. . . .

I'd compare learning short game shots to learning to play the guitar or the piano. You can learn some basic fundamentals that work for simple songs, and add to those fundamentals slowly to become a more talented player. And just like music, the short game and putting are "art" forms that you can appreciate by watching, but you get more in terms of instruction by going out and experimenting yourself.

My whole goal with this book is to help you reinforce the basic framework of your short game and putting—the musical chords, if you will—and start to visualize more of the possibilities for the different short game situations that come up. I certainly don't believe in taking a cookie-cutter approach to short game shotmaking: I believe you should pick the shot that is the best combination of a good choice for the situation and a good fit for your skill set.

Take the ideas from the previous nine chapters—summarized here in the quick reference guide—and go out to your home course and experiment. You might find that certain parts of what I'm talking about click more than others. That's just fine. If I can give you one or two more "go-to" shots to improve your chances of getting up and down, I think that's going to help you enjoy your golf more.

BASIC PITCH SHOT

- The stance is square to the target line (not open), and slightly narrower than standard.
- The grip should be neutral, with the V's created by the thumbs and the sides of the hands pointing at the right collarbone.
- When setting the grip, be sure to hold the club in the fingers—not across the palms, which restricts wrist action.
- The narrower stance promotes lower-body rotation—the key to a successful pitch. You don't want to feel as though your legs are encased in concrete.
- Your feet, knees, hips, and shoulders should all be parallel to the target line. The tendency is to open the stance and keep the shoulders square, a position that produces inconsistent contact.
- The shaft should be set neutral—straight up and down—not leaned forward, toward the target.
- Weight distribution is 65 to 70 percent on the left foot at address, and it should stay there during the swing.
- Avoid letting the right shoulder get low at address—this is a symptom of trying to help the ball into the air by scooping at it.
- In the swing, the hands stay close to the body and the weight of the clubhead generates all the energy.

BASIC BUNKER SHOT

- Set up square to the target, not open as commonly taught.

- The clubface should be square or just slightly open.
- Spread your feet wide—wider than driver width—and tilt your spine to the left, toward the target. Bend your knees to get lower to the ground, almost as if you were preparing to sit in a chair.
- The ball should be positioned in the center of your stance, and the shaft should be leaned back, away from the target—this exposes more of the bounce on the bottom of the club.
- The swing is essentially the cocking of the wrists up and down—it's almost as if you're setting the club on first your right shoulder and then on your left while adding an upper-body turn.
- Keep your hands close to your body and feel a cup in the top of your left wrist on both the backswing and the follow-through.
- Splash the sand two inches behind the ball.

LAG PUTTING

- Solid contact in the middle of the putterface is the most important element to good lag putting, because it really dials in speed control.
- In the grip, start with the palms opposing each other and perpendicular to the target line.
- I prefer the reverse overlap grip, where the left index finger extends over the knuckles of the right hand.
- The shaft of the putter should run in a line with the arms.
- Stance is shoulder-width, with the feet, knees, hips, and shoulders square to the target line.

- The most important alignment position is the top of the forearms. If the shoulders are out of position, a line on top of the forearms won't run parallel to the target line. If the forearms are out of alignment, you'll have to use your hands to compensate.
- To set your posture, tilt forward from the hips, don't slump your spine. If you slump, your arms can't swing freely in front of you.
- When you tilt, your eyes should look down just inside the ball. To measure, take your stance, hold a ball between your eyes, and drop it. It should hit just inside the ball on the ground.
- At address, your elbows should feel "soft" and sit lightly against your rib cage.
- Ball position is center, and the stroke should feel as though your right elbow is sliding back against your ribs, followed by the left sliding back into place along your ribs on the other side.
- Stay connected to your read by stepping into your stance and making your stroke within ten seconds.
- A consistent putting stroke takes the same amount of time no matter how long the putt is. On a longer putt, the stroke is longer and faster. On a short stroke, it's shorter and slower.

MID-RANGE PITCH

- Control distance on awkward-length pitches with the speed of your pivot, not by increasing or decreasing your arm swing. A bigger, faster pivot will make the ball go farther.

- The wrists and forearms control this shot's trajectory. Do not change your ball position. To hit the ball lower, bow the left wrist (as though you were hitting a topspin ping-pong shot) through impact.

IN THE ROUGH, CLOSE TO THE HOLE

- Deep grass behaves much like bunker sand. If you can see the ball in the grass, you can play a shot very similar to a standard bunker shot and get good results.
- The way the grass sits has an impact on shot selection. If you're close to where short grass starts, you have the option to use a putter or a hybrid with a putting stroke.
- No matter what shot you choose, be sure to make some body pivot. A common mistake on a short shot is to keep the body completely still and stab at the ball with the arms, a move that usually produces a bladed shot across the green.

LONG BUNKER SHOT

- Standard "blast" bunker shots max out at about 25 to 30 yards.
- For a bunker shot longer than that distance, switch to a standard pitch or chip stance.
- Instead of hitting the sand behind the ball, hit the ball first in an intentionally skulled chip.

- Play the ball slightly back of center, hit the ball first, and control distance with the size of your pivot.
- This shot will roll out, so you have to account for that roll.

TROUBLE

- The default shot from a bad lie is a standard bunker-style shot with the bounce of the club hitting behind the ball. This shot will produce decent results from almost any trouble location.
- Read the grass in the rough to determine what kind of shot options you have. If the grass is lying in the same direction as your intended shot, the ball will probably jump out of the grass. If the grass is running against your ball, you risk getting the club tangled in the rough unless you play a shot with more speed. If the ball sits on top of the grass, be careful not to swing below the ball and miss it. In this situation, a conservative chip is a good play.
- If the ball sits on the front edge of a divot, you can play a normal variety of shots because you can make clean contact with the ball. If the ball is in the back of the divot, the club will make inconsistent contact with the ball because of the irregular ground, so a bunker-style shot is the best play.
- From a downhill lie, the tendency is to hang back to try to help the ball into the air, both from the rough and the sand. Keep your spine tilted toward the hole, widen your stance, and move your right foot back,

away from the target line. This will help you make a steeper swing into the ball.

- To get more height on a bunker shot, open the club-face, angle the shaft more away from the target, and lower your hands. The lower your hands are at address, the higher the ball will go.
- When under pressure, fixate on the process, not the outcome. Have a standard pre-putt routine that you always go through, and take the same amount of time for every shot. If you can lose yourself in the process—and be satisfied no matter what happens, as long as you followed the process—you'll improve under pressure.

SHORT GAME STRATEGY

- Diagnose a hole from green to tee. Where are the worst places to be? Water, out-of-bounds, tough up-and-downs, etc. Plot backward to avoid those places at all costs.
- Visualize a map of each green complex with an overlay—green areas around the green are safe places to miss, yellow areas are sketchy, and red areas are dead. If you do miss a green, the goal is to miss in the green areas.
- "Leave" is a crucial concept in the short game and putting. As important as it is to try to get the ball close to (or in) the hole with a short game shot or a putt, it's just as important to leave a miss in the easiest place to approach the next shot. When putting, that means understanding that being six feet away

but straight up the hill is better than being three feet away but with a downhill, sidehill breaker.

- Reading greens is something you do by acquiring a lot of information and weighing it. For example, by surveying the overall green complex and finding the place where the green drains, you'll know that putts will tend to break toward that low point. If a natural creek or pond runs next to a green, putts will tend to break toward the water.
- To make an accurate read, identify the high point of the break—the apex of the curve the ball will roll on—and set yourself up to aim at that spot. The tendency is to subtly cheat your aim toward the hole. Walk to the low side of the putt, halfway between the ball and the hole, to get the best view of the line.
- Fast, downhill putts are much more sensitive to break, because the ball is traveling much more slowly. Uphill putts are hit with more speed, which neutralizes some break.
- Green speed is a function of two factors—the length of the grass and the hardness of the ground beneath the grass. If the grass is long and the ground is moist, the greens will be slow, and vice versa.
- Green speed can change from hole to hole, depending on how exposed the green is to the wind. Wind dries off surface moisture, making the greens quicker.
- Grain is a factor on most putts, not just those on Bermuda-grass greens. You can judge how strong the grain is by checking to see if the grass looks shiny from one side. On a strong-grain green, a ten-footer that would otherwise have been straight can move as much as three or four inches off line if it is across the grain. To see which direction the grain goes, check

the cup. The grass grows away from the clean side of the hole and toward the ragged side.

- Sand firmness dictates how far behind the ball you can hit from the bunker. The firmer the sand, the closer you can hit to the ball—and the more spin you'll produce.
- From firm sand, you can make a slower swing, because less sand is being displaced between the club and the ball.
- To test the firmness of the sand, pay attention to how your shoes react when you step into the bunker. If you stay on top of the sand, like a wet beach, it's obviously firm. It's common for sand to have a crusty layer on top but be fluffy underneath, especially in the morning when the dew is still out. Treat this sand as fluffy.

EQUIPMENT

- The three main characteristics of your short game clubs are loft, bounce, and lie angle.
- Loft is the measure of how high and far a club will hit the ball. A club with more loft, like a 58-degree wedge, will hit the ball higher and shorter than a 20-degree 3-iron.
- Bounce angle is the amount of material that hangs below the leading edge of the wedge. Like loft, it's measured in degrees. Most lofted wedges range from three degrees of bounce (not very much) to 16 degrees (a big flange).
- Lie angle is how upright or flat the clubhead is built in relation to the shaft. The closer you stand to the

ball, either because of your setup or because of your build, the more upright the club should be. In general, I think wedges should be built with a slightly flatter lie angle than standard (52 degrees instead of 54), because I teach a flatter short game swing.

- The goal is to have a collection of wedges that covers the variety of full and short shots you need to hit.
- I use a 58-degree wedge with 12 degrees of bounce, a 52-degree gap wedge with eight degrees of bounce, and a 48-degree pitching wedge. I chose the gaps between my wedges based on how far I hit each club from the fairway.
- I hit virtually all my short game shots with my 58--degree wedge. It's easier to learn how to adapt one club to a variety of different shots than to judge distance with a lot of different clubs.
- The playing characteristics of wedges are easy to change. Clubfitters can easily bend a wedge to give it more or less loft, or a more upright or flatter lie angle. I even had some of the bounce shaved off the heel of my 58-degree wedge so I can lay the club flatter on the ground from tight lies if I need to.

CHARTING

- Keep some simple-to-record statistics on your own short game to get a much clearer picture of what you actually do on and around the greens. Measure how far away you are from the hole on every full-swing approach shot you hit. Then make a notation about where the shot ended up—on the green (G), in the rough (R), on the fringe (F), in a bunker (B), or out of play (O).

- Measure the distance you have from the hole after hitting each short game shot from 30 yards off the green or closer. When you look at this total, you'll get a strong sense of two things—how good your chipping, pitching, and sand games are, and how difficult the short game shots you're leaving yourself are.

- Count the number of total putts you take for the round. Once you make your first putt, measure how far you are away from the cup. If you have a tap-in, call it one foot. From that measurement, you can determine both an average second-putt length and the total feet of putts you have.

ACKNOWLEDGMENTS

The idea for *The Art of Scoring* came from playing a fun round of golf with two friends, Tom Headley and Hugh Illsley. Tom was facing an interesting shot, and I offered my opinion on a different option than the one he was considering. Tom got up and down, and he turned on a light bulb when he joked that he knew what book I ought to do next.

I have to say that there wouldn't be any "next" book without my friend Matt Rudy. Matt helped me write *The Art of Putting* and *The Art of the Short Game*, along with a dozen articles for *Golf Digest,* where he's a senior writer. We dreamed up the idea for a scoring "situations book," but he came up with the structure and asked me the right questions so we could come up with the right answers. And just like he did with the first two books, J. D. Cuban makes me look way better in photographs than I do in real life. Scott Waxman and Farley Chase got me a great deal with Gotham, and teamed me up with a talented editor there, Jessica Sindler. Thanks as well to Robert Kraut of Booklegger for his continuing support.

In addition to being a part of that playing group with Tom, Hugh has played an important role in my development as a teacher. He sat me down and asked me where I'd rank myself as a player. Then he asked me where I'd rank myself as a putting instructor. When I answered those questions, it became a lot clearer where I should be spending my time. I haven't played many tournaments since we had that talk, but my income has gone up drastically. It helps to have good friends looking out for you.

I want to say thanks to my dad, Frank Utley, who became a golf fanatic when I was ten years old. He was my first coach, and he taught me how to think, both on the golf course and off. My mom, Ruby, taught me patience and positive thinking. My brother John has been a best friend forever and is now the ultimate business associate.

I've had a lot of great teachers over the years—from Ken Lanning back when I was a kid to Jim Parkins, Rich Poe, and Brian Allen during my college years. Craig Harrison, Fred Griffin, and Rob Akins have helped a lot along the way as well. Jim Hardy has really become my mentor over the last five or six years—not only in terms of understanding my own game, but in helping me be a better teacher.

I also owe a lot of what I've become as a teacher to the friends I made as a player. Dillard Pruitt, Fred Wadsworth, and Brandel Chamblee were my running buddies when I turned pro, and we played a lot of practice rounds and ate a lot of bad food together. They're lifelong friends. And Tom Pernice was generous enough to show me the bunker technique I'm teaching to this day. He's a good man.

I have to thank my wife, Elayna, more than anyone. She's been my partner, my wife, my coach, and my best friend. I certainly couldn't have had the career I've had without her help.

I also want to acknowledge my Lord and Savior—the giver of great gifts, who has given me the passion to encourage others not just to know Him, but to know and understand golf a little bit better.

ABOUT THE AUTHOR

STAN UTLEY has been a professional golfer on the PGA Tour since 1989, and has earned more than $1 million in prize money. Voted one of America's Top 10 Greatest Teachers by *Golf Digest,* he has set records for his short game play, and his student list includes fellow pros such as Jay Haas, Paul McGinley, Peter Jacobsen, Graeme McDowell, Dudley Hart, Omar Uresti, Mike Weir, and Sergio Garcia. He lives in Scottsdale, Arizona.

MATTHEW RUDY is a senior writer for *Golf Digest* and has coauthored books and articles with Ernie Els, Phil Mickelson, Johnny Miller, and Hank Haney, among other players and teachers. He lives in Fairfield, Connecticut.